Communication policies in the **Federal Republic of Germany**

In this series

Communication policies in the **Federal Republic of Germany**

A study carried out by the
Arbeitsgemeinschaft für Kommunikationsforschung
and written by
Walter A. Mahle and Rolf Richter

The Unesco Press
Paris 1974

Published by the Unesco Press,
7 Place de Fontenoy, 75700 Paris
Printed by S.C. Maison d'Édition, Marcinelle (Belgium)

ISBN 92-3-101184-7
French edition: 92-3-201184-0

Preface

Communication policies are sets of principles and norms established to guide the behaviour of communication systems. They are shaped over time in the context of society's general approach to communication and to the media. Emanating from political ideologies, the social and economic conditions of the country and the values on which they are based, they strive to relate these to the real needs for and the prospective opportunities of communication.

Communication policies exist in every society, though they may sometimes be latent and disjointed, rather than clearly articulated and harmonized. They may be very general, in the nature of desirable goals and principles, or they may be more specific and practically binding. They may exist or be formulated at many levels. They may be incorporated in the constitution or legislation of a country; in over-all national policies, in the guidelines for individual administrations, in professional codes of ethics as well as in the constitutions and operational rules of particular communication institutions.

The publication of this series of studies has been undertaken as part of the programme adopted by the General Conference of Unesco at its sixteenth session, related to the analysis of communication policies as they exist at the different levels—public, institutional, professional—in selected countries. The aim of the series is to present this information in a manner which can be comparable. Thus an attempt has been made to follow, as far as possible, a fairly similar structural pattern and method of approach which was agreed between the national institutions undertaking the work.

Within this series of monographs the first five studies are devoted to European communication policies of Hungary, Ireland, Sweden, Federal Republic of Germany and Yugoslavia. Similar studies for Latin America are in progress in Brazil, Colombia, Costa Rica and Peru. These will be followed by policies studies carried out in Asian countries.

This study was carried out by the Arbeitsgemeinschaft für Kommunikationsforschung, in Munich, and written by Walter A. Mahle and Rolf Richter. Assistance with specialist sections was given by co-workers as follows: Wolfgang R. Langenbucher (Sect. 6); Andreas Meyer (Sect. 3.3); Helga Montag (Sect. 8.1); and Susanne Welzel (Sect. 8.2). Walter A. Mahle was responsible for Sections 1, 2.1, 4, and 7; Rolf Richter for Sections 2.2, 3.1, 3.2, and 5. Kent O. Döring made the translation into English.

The opinions expressed by the authors do not necessarily reflect the views of Unesco.

Contents

1 Observations and hypotheses on the concept of communication policies

The concept of communication policies has only recently arisen although the facts and actions that it describes are thousands of years old: 'Communication policies are as old as politics themselves.'[1] The development of communication policies into a separate field appears to refer to social problems arising out of increasingly complex communications. Previously small communication problems have, in fact or appearance, grown into substantial ones. But, they are at least now seen as such and are gaining proportionate public attention. A few of the mass media structural problems in the Federal Republic of Germany which have caused such developments are enumerated in Chapters 2 and 3, and run through the other chapters like a red thread.

There has been amplified discussion of communication policies in recent years, especially in the political parties. Despite this, a final, precise and bindingly acceptable definition of communication policies has yet to be made.[2] Therefore, a short outline of the problem will be given in the following pages. The outline conveys the clearly subjective preferences of the author, and thus no claims are made to cover all or only the most important positions in the discussion.

The discussion should proceed on a definition of 'communication policies' as the 'totality of measures by the State and social organisations [institutions and groups should also be included to complete this (author)] directed at regulating the processes of social communication'.[3] One point in this definition appears especially important to me and is therefore worth accentuating: the State is not exclusively active in communication policies, nor should it be according to the constitution of the Federal Republic of Germany.

1. Otto B. Rögele, in *Fischer Lexikon, Publizistik*, p. 76, Frankfurt am Main, 1971.
2. The lack of an adequate definition is probably due to essential problems remaining open and unsolved in the discussion. On the other hand, other narrower or wider definitions which are seen as politically proper are made in the context of respective political programmes. In the linguistics of natural science, the designation function and the semantics of a concept stand, or should stand in the foreground. But, the gravity of a term in political usage often lies only in the pragmatic dimension. In other words, the problem is not one of merely reaching agreement on the term 'communication policies' as a specific denotation, but with seeing its connotations and varied usage as it is usually conjoined with certain normative and political objectives. This naturally hinders any binding agreements about the denotations and connotations of the term.
3. Peter Glotz, in Kurt Koszyk and Karl Hugo Pruys, *dtv-Woerterbuch zur Publizistik*, p. 185, Munich, 1969.

However, the broad definition quoted above hardly corresponds to the usual definitions of communication policies as used in political discussions. It is possible that these can be consequently outlined as 'intentional political activities by State and other socially active groups which are primarily intended to regulate communication'.

In actual discussion, 'media policies' is more often used than 'communication policies'. Which of the terms is the more useful and correct? A very pragmatic argument would be that the term 'communication policies' has been internationally introduced, and is thus internationally useful. I further believe that this term is more inclusive and accurate for other reasons. One argument is that pure 'media policies' are not restricted to the media. Regulation of the media also extensively reaches into other areas of social communications and influences and regulates these in indirect ways, regardless and independent of any intention.[1] A second argument for the term 'communication policies' may be derived out of the political communication activities which have developed until now. Although there have been earlier political media activities, the term is new. Equally true, there were, and are, political activities which also include, or exclusively relate to, non-media communications and regulate them. Good examples thereof are the legal regulations and restrictions upon the freedom of assembly, or the political initiatives for establishing community centres of communication. It therefore seems sensible to include these areas under the general term of 'communication policies'.

Such a view would seem apparently unusual because it partially contradicts historical experience: communication policies as intentional communication policy activity usually relates exclusively to the 'media' in countries with a 'Western' democratic tradition. Other communication forms are treated rarely as political matters and even then usually under some aspect other than that of communications. One is less conscious that the latter are regulated along with the former.

On the other hand, it may be demonstrated that the communication policies of totalitarian States envelop or attempt to contain practically all means of social communication all the way down to gossip and private communication as seen, for example, in the control of private correspondence.

This leads to the respective questions of if, why, when and where communication policies may be necessary. The following general hypothesis has been formulated as a provisional answer:

The necessity for intentional communication policies always arises when social communication is no longer self evident, no longer functions in a self-evident manner and becomes questionable and unreliable, or when it produces dysfunctional results in the communications system which extend to the social system. This applies not only to the media, but to non-media communications as well.

1. This is based on the recognition that the social communication process arises out of a highly complex interplay between media and non-media forms of communication. Political regulation of communications directed at the mass media thus indirectly influences and regulates even non-media communications, and that often without intention.

Such a concept is diametrically opposed by the widespread position that extensively or totally rejects communication policies. Such a position that is extremely sceptical about all communication policies may have essentially two reasons or causes. First, there is the historical and actual experience with totalitarian control of all communication forms. Fresh memories of these experiences automatically raise suspicion in the Federal Republic of Germany that communication policy planning may mean a relapse to totalitarian control. An indication for this hypothesis can be seen in the numerous quests to find parallels between the present political communication activities and those of the Third Reich with its Editorial Law, Reich's Press Chamber, etc., thus devaluating and rejecting post-war communication policies.

It seems to me that a second reason for the scepticism about communication policies is to be found in the classical liberal economic and socio-political concepts which still play a stronger role here than in other political areas. It is argued that a self regulation of social communication is always to be preferred over communication policy measures, especially those of the State.

This scepticism is contrary to the experience that a non-regulated communications market does not necessarily establish an optimum of freedom of communication for all, or even the requisite functional minimums thereof, and it may even endanger it. In so far as this is the case, planned communication policies appear necessary, and even State communication policies may become legitimate in extreme cases. Truly, this is not to subjugate social communications to State influence, but to maintain and improve equal communication chances for all.

It is only in this sense which excludes regimentation and every form of censorship that democratic communication policies can be legitimate, necessary and meaningful as a structural policy. We can speak here of a concept of social communications freedom in contrast to the liberal, individualistic freedom of belief.

The question if communication policy extends only to the media or if it may also consider and regulate non-media communication has already been partially answered by the above-mentioned examples where they are already occuring. The following empirical hypothesis should supplement this:

Traditional forms of non-media communication have been lost with traditional forms of social life, or have at least lost their main function and meaning. This can be illustrated by reference to two key words: the village and the neighbourhood. Both structures have either disappeared or been radically altered due to the growing mobility and urbanization of a greater proportion of the population. The large family or clan that includes several generations has been largely displaced by the small family unit with only one or two generations. The resulting problems such as 'old-age ghettos', urban isolation, etc., are also primary problems of communication.

Structural weakness in the area of non-media communication has become especially conspicuous in the unseen results of urban planning and development. There are large communities and cities for thousands which have been planned,

11

built and occupied in a few short years. They fulfil the occupants's physical needs, but almost totally neglect their communication needs. Good symbols for the neglect of human communication needs are the so-called 'grass widows' in the bedroom suburbs and socially disturbed children in the satellite cities.

That a deficit in community communications exists and that a necessity for non-media communications planning is recognized now, may be seen in the efforts to create community centres of communication in Sweden and the Federal Republic of Germany. The informal, non-media communication structures which grew up in the past decades and centuries with the development of communities cannot naturally grow to match the pace of modern urban development. The needed community communication structures can only arise when urban planning includes communication policy as well, and that in a much broader sense than the previous connotations of the term.

Large-scale communication problems do not solely exist in the new satellite settlements. This is revealed in empirically proved relationships such as urban anonymity, the lack of social contacts, the lack of interpersonal communication contacts, alienation and criminality.

The relationship of 'the more media usage, the less outward, active social contact' finally shows directly how media communications can adversely influence non-media forms of communication.

All of these examples illustrate that both an isolated view of the media, and a neglect of non-media communications in establishing communication policies have been unrealistic and therefore false. This leads to the hypothesis that as soon as the self-regulating mechanisms of non-media social communication no longer function adequately, communication policy measures could become essential.

The insight that social communication occurs through a very complex interchange of different media and non-media communications has been supported by the results of empirical research. It has recently gained further circulation and is even entering into the discussion of communication policy. Certain conclusions may be drawn from this view.

First, communication policy should not confine itself to any one medium. The heading 'Common Market of the media' is coming into usage and better indicates how the media must be considered when something in one sector of the communication system must be regulated. In contrast to that, past communication policy has been largely without any guiding conceptions: it has been re-aligned with each new, specific problem and symptom, and has too often ignored other important factors, the interplay with other media, or the effects that it may have had on them.

Secondly, communication policy may not restrict itself to the media. It must refer to and consider the effects of media policy measures on non-media communication more extensively than it has in the past. Even intentional communication policies for non-media areas such as urban planning and education will become indispensable in the long run. This has been extensively established above.

Thirdly, communication policy must increasingly consider the public in addition to the media, its organization and its personnel. This, because communication policy may not be solely prepared for the media offerings without considering how the public actually uses them now, and how it may use them in the future. The selective behaviour of the recipient, his overlapping and complementary use of the media, his time budget, his use of the accepted information, etc., are facts which are only partially formed by media content. They may in no way be politically 'regulated', but they must be investigated as relatively stable and decisive factors in the communication process when making communication policy decisions if the latter are not to be unrealistic.

Until recently, the question of communication conditions has been discussed and decided almost exclusively from their economic and juridical aspects. The communications and political aspects are only now coming slowly to the fore. The understanding that arose with the term 'communication policy' and the tendencies indicated in it are now being included in the political area.

This is most clearly revealed by the communication policy concepts or even the over-all concepts that are being often advanced today. Singular and unco-ordinated communication policy measures are increasingly found to be insufficient as there is an often proved and criticized deficit in their objectives. This is demonstrated by the major political parties having advanced so-called 'media papers' in which they laid down their communication policy programmes.[1]

The question remains fully open as to what is to be understood by a communication policy concept, or general concept, and what the conditions for it may be. It should be discussed shortly here. Contrary to short-term, specific measures, a general communication policy concept is to be understood as a co-ordinating and long-term structural policy. According to the above, it may take a separate view of each of the different media, but must consider their reciprocal interrelationship and dependence. A general concept must also consider non-media communication forms and solve the problems in that area. And, an essentially stronger orientation to audience behaviour and behaviour possibilities would be indispensable for any comprehensive problem analyses and realistic solutions based upon them.

The formulation of a general concept will only be possible when a normative socio-political model has been established from which a model communication policy concept can be drawn. This then formulates objectives for communication policy and objective priorities. Further, priorities of various value areas must be considered because a development of conflicts between various value areas such as economic v. communication freedom may not be avoided, conflicts which can only be decided by a balanced consideration of all the essentials.

An equally important condition is a substance analysis of communication realities, that is, a stocktaking of the actual functions and effects of the media, etc. It is thus the only way that unsure and unfounded communication policy

1. cf. Chapter 7.

decisions with unknown results and side effects can be progressively replaced by systematic measures with a controllable degree of risk and success.

Normative models and factual analyses cannot be separated: normative models condition the type and direction of the factual analyses. Their results in turn can test, modify and correct the normative hypotheses' validity. However, a certain asymmetry can develop in the political realities. Our knowledge will often be insufficient to solve threatening problems to the communications order. Communication policy decisions are thus forced which are based on unsure knowledge and which carry risks and insecurity in them.

We further need a set of communication policy instruments for any general concept, an instrumental set to take inventory of those means at our disposal and those which can be developed. This merges with the reflection as to which means are best adapted to solving certain problems with the least possible intervention. Therewith, the questions are especially important as to what the intended results of the means are and, above all, what the unintended side effects may be.

A few inferences may be made from the observations and postulates that have been mentioned here. A general concept appears to be necessary when structural weaknesses arise which cannot be solved by specific, partial regulations. If such abstract values are to be achieved, they must come from theory–reality comparisons. However, they would still remain controversial according to the underlying differences between normative hypotheses and factual analyses.

Further, a general concept should be realized only in the measure that both the intended results as well as the unintended side effects are fairly predictable, and if their risks can be calculated to some degree.

Our factual knowledge remains insufficient in most areas of the problem. Just as in other previously developed objective postulates, the normative hypothesis is neither precise and developed enough nor sufficiently examined as to its desirability and feasibility as to allow an immediate formulation of a general concept.

Existing media papers are primary attempts and steps in the direction of fulfilling the continuing and growing demand for a general communication policy concept. According to one's political outlook, it may be more a question of an orientation model, or that of a performance model with an extensive catalogue of communication policy measures.

The understanding of communication policy that has been sketched here should be finally summarized in the form of several postulates and hypotheses:

The more complex society becomes, and the less a communications system functions in a self-evident and self-regulating manner, the more essential an intentional and systematic communication policy becomes in the sense of ordering structural policy. However, such structural policy may not restrict social communications freedom in any way. It should, instead, make the conditions available for its best possible development. Different social groups, organizations and institutions, not primarily the State, can be representative agents of communication policy. But, even a democratic State will increasingly see the necessity of aiding the claim of each individual to an equal chance at participating in the process of social communication.

2 Media and communication policies in the Federal Republic of Germany

2.1 Outline of the underlying structure

Before going into detail about the development and problems of the communication policies in the Federal Republic of Germany, it would be appropriate if some short introductory comments were made about the underlying structures.

THE POLITICAL SYSTEM

The Federal Republic of Germany is a federally structured democratic-parliamentarian State. The Federal Parliament comprises two chambers, the Bundestag (the Federal Parliament) and the Bundesrat (the Federal Council).

The Bundestag is directly elected every four years by the total population. Half of the approximately 500 members of parliament are personally elected, the other half are indirectly elected from party lists.

The Bundesrat is the representation of the eleven *Länder* (including West Berlin). According to the population of the *Länder*, the *Land* governments send three to five representatives to the Bundesrat which at present has forty-five members.

According to the republic's constitution, legislative authority rests principally with the *Länder*, and with the federation only where specifically provided for in the constitution. The cultural authority, and with it communication policy authority, falls extensively under the legislative jurisdiction of the member *Länder*. The federation has here almost only a frame authority, that is, the possibility to regulate general legal relationships but not in detail.

THE PRESS

The press in the Federal Republic of Germany is almost exclusively organized in private business. At the present time there are just over 500 daily and weekly newspapers with a cumulative press run of approximately 21 million copies each issue (1973). The number of newspapers with a completely autonomous editorial staff which produces its total editorial content has sunk from 225 in 1954 to about 130 in 1973.

In addition to the daily and weekly newspapers, there are about 230 popular magazines which appear either weekly, bi-weekly or monthly and which have a cumulative press run of about 63 million copies each issue (1973).[1]

Complementing the above are innumerable school, office and professional publications, circulars, customer and house magazines. The number of professional magazines alone is estimated to be much more than 10,000 titles.

RADIO AND TELEVISION BROADCASTING

Post-war German radio and television broadcasting has, until now, been exclusively organized under public ownership and control, and extensively corresponds to the federal political structure. This is described in detail in Chapter 8.[2]

MEDIA AVAILABILITY AND MEDIA USE (1970)[3]

Out of every 100 households in the Federal Republic eighty-five have a television, ninety-five have a radio and seventy-seven subscribe to or regularly purchase a newspaper.

In an average work day, the following (out of 100 people over 14 years at age) will be reached by: television, 72; radio, 67; daily newspapers, 70.

These three media together reach an average of 95 per cent of the population on an average work day.

The average media use per work day totals 3.5 hours. The tendency is growing, and this is exclusively attributable to the growing use of television.

2.2 A summary of post-war communication policy developments in the Federal Republic of Germany

As a result of the Second World War and the subsequent occupation of Germany by the Allied powers, the occupying powers assumed responsibility for communication policies in their respective zones in the years from 1945 to 1949. Since the summer of 1945, shortly after occupation, the Allies distributed licences to issue newspapers and magazines to select individuals whom the Allies believed would guarantee an anti-fascist position in their publications. The essential end of the Allies' press policies in the three western zones, the area of the present Federal Republic, was the creation of a democratic, politically balanced and extensively regional press, although the means partially differed in each zone.

The very strict controls that the Allies placed upon these publications were gradually loosened. In the autumn of 1945, the American military government even lifted prior censorship, and the British and French soon followed suit.

1. For the development of press run figures in the newspapers and magazine industries, see Appendix.
2. cf. also facts and figures given in the appendix.
3. Results of a research poll taken by Infratest: *Massenkommunikation* 1964-70, Munich, 1970. Details in *Media Perspektiven*, No. 156, 1971 and Nos. 2, 4, 5, 6, 1972.

In October 1947, the British turned over the licence distribution for their zone to the ministers-president of the *Länder* (states) in it, and who were advised by a zone press council and state press committees. The latter were composed of representatives from the journalists, the publishers and the general public. Press laws enacted in 1948–49 by the north German *Länder* provided for similar committees.

All responsibility for communication policy was handed back to German authorities after the constitution of the Federal Republic of Germany was approved by the *Länder* in 1949. Article 5 of the constitution guarantees freedom of the press, and as the constitution went into effect, those journalists and publishers who had been prohibited by the Allies from practising because of press activities during the period between 1933 and 1945 were again able to practise their trade.

There was a similar situation in broadcasting. In 1945, the Allies impounded all of the Third Reich's radio transmitters. However, they turned over broadcasting authority to the *Länder* even before the promulgation of the constitution. Since the beginning of 1948, the State created broadcasting institutes in the Federal Republic, either by state laws, or by interstate treaties if the broadcasting area included several *Länder*. However, the Allies retained the right to participate in the formulation of these laws and treaties, especially as regards the organizational forms of the broadcasting institutes.[1]

The Allies also influenced the legislation of press acts. After a 1946 press bill for all of the states in the American zone was rejected by the occupying authority, press acts were passed in 1948–49, under the Allies supervision, in the *Länder* of the present Federal Republic with the exception of Niedersachsen, Saarland and Rheinland-Pfalz.

A 1952 attempt by the federation to pass a press 'frame' or 'skeleton' law[2] failed, mostly because of the opposition by the press organisations. And, although there has been subsequent discussion of the matter and several drafts made by the press organizations and the Sozialdemokratische Partei Deutschlands (SPD) and Frei Demokratische Partei (FDP) fractions in the Bundestag (Federal Parliament), no such 'press frame law' has been enacted.

Since 1952, the communication policies of the federation remained focused upon broadcasting as well as specific singular problems of the press. Attempts by the federal government to gain more influence upon broadcasting by the passage of a federal broadcasting law and by negotiations with the *Länder* were undone by the latters' opposition.

Discussion of press politics in the early fifties centred on problems which, in the framework of the federation's general legislative activities, were relevent to the press: especially management participation, disclosure of State secrets, the right of a witness to refuse testimony, press impoundment, the information obligation of public authorities and the protection of minors.

---

1. cf. Chapter 8.
2. A federal 'skeleton' or 'frame' law is a federally legislated outline of laws that are to be both legislated in detail and executed by the member *Länder*.

Efforts by the press organizations to create institutions of self-control fell into this period. In 1954, the magazine publishers had already founded such a voluntary organ of self-control with an eye on the protection of minors. This establishment had a turbulent fate and ended its activities in 1971 because of internal discord.[1]

In the autumn of 1956, representatives of the publishers' and journalists' organizations founded the German Press Council which is patterned after the British Press Council. It was at first composed of five publishers and an equal number of journalists from the daily press. It was extended in 1957 to include ten representatives from the magazine press and exists in this form at present.[2]

The conflict between the broadcasting institutes and the newspaper publishers over broadcasting advertising began in the mid-fifties. The publishers disputed the right of the institutes to broadcast advertising, because this was supposedly in conflict with their legitimate public construction. A suit brought by the publishers' association against the Bavarian Broadcasting System, which first introduced television advertising, was decided in 1957 in favour of the broadcasting institute. The Munich Court of Appeals confirmed the right of the broadcasting institutes to broadcast advertising in so far as its contents do not endanger the state of a diverse press. However, this question has been further determined by political communication policy discussion.

In 1957, the federation touched off a long and intense public debate by seizing an initiative in the area of libel law. Equally controversial, the federal government attempted to gain influence on television by moving to found a national television network. Since its beginnings in the Federal Republic, this medium has been exclusively regulated by the broadcasting laws of the individual *Länder*. In 1961, the federation was forced to drop its already extensive preparations for the network by a judgement of the Federal Constitutional Court. The second German television network (ZDF) which eventually came into being is also operated by the *Länder*.

The 'television judgement' also ended attempts by the publishers, pressed since the mid-fifties, to gain access to this medium. Publishers and other businessmen had previously called a private production company into life while counting on co-operation with the federal network, and had thus made extensive preparations by the time the company dissolved itself in 1961.

However, the publishers persevered in their claims to be included in broadcasting. At the same time, they increasingly stressed that the existence of a free press was endangered by rising advertising broadcasting by public broadcasting. The Bundestag asked the federal government to institute an independent commission of scientists to examine the publishers' complaint. After years of inquiry, the commission concluded in 1967 that both the publishers' complaint and their claims were unfounded in fact.

By this time, both attempts by the newspaper publishers to take over the programme productions of the second German television channel (ZDF) and

1. cf. Section 4.1.
2. cf. Section 4.2.

their legal initiative to ban advertising by public broadcasters had already fallen through in 1964 and 1967 respectively.

The press was more successful in putting its interests through in *Länder* press laws initiated and passed between 1959 and 1966. The same was true of certain conditions in the 1968 National Emergency Act which were applicable to the press, and for treason paragraphs in amendments to the national legal code enacted in the same year.

The problem of 'internal press freedom' which was discussed in the immediate post-war years was resuscitated in 1959–60, and with it the controversies over the separation of authority between the publishers and editorial staffs, and over the management participation of the staff in publishing and business decisions. However, the demands raised by the journalists' organizations found immediate resonance with neither the political decision makers nor the publishers. Collective bargaining on those points has been only entered into since 1968.

The question at the centre of the conflict was how far should a publisher go beyond his authority to establish the basic position of a paper into the right of deciding specific editorial questions. There was also the problem of staff participation in personnel decisions directly affecting it.

The negotiations led to a 1970 agreement for drafting a contract between the press organizations. However, this agreement was rejected by one of the journalists' organizations as being too friendly to the publishers. Since then, new negotiations have been entered into, especially as the federal government is pressing for the conclusion of such a contract with a planned press 'frame' law.

In the meanwhile, several publishers had agreed to introduce editorial statutes dealing with the same questions, and which, in part, extensively meet the demands of the journalists.

The so-called 'statute movement' has even spread to the broadcasting institutions where statute drafts have been drafted for all of the institutions, and editorial committees have been formed to represent the interests of the journalists. However, none of these statutes have been yet formally recognized by the institutes.[1]

Parallel to the area 'internal press freedom', there has been the problem of press concentration which has been accelerating since the mid-sixties. Despite a rise in total circulation, this concentration has led to a reduction of the number of fully autonomous editorial staffs from 213 in 1962 to approximately 130 in 1973. At the same time, the number of 'one newspaper areas' with only one regional or local daily newspaper rose to about one-third of the total area in the Federal Republic.

Under the pressure of these developments, the federal government instituted an examining commission in May 1967 which was composed of representatives from the press, broadcasting and the general public. It quickly presented recommendations for immediate corrective action, and, in 1968, presented an

---

1. cf. Section 8.2; in the meanwhile, one statute (NDR) has been recognized.

extensive report recommending a long-term structural policy for the press. While it is true that the federal government only took up a small fraction of those recommendations, state and federal governments, parliaments and the general public are more deeply examining the problems of the mass media.

3 Public communication policies

3.1 The communication policies of the German federation, 1949-72

According to Article 75, section 2, of the Federal Republic of Germany's 1949 constitution, the federation has the right to pass federal 'frame' or 'skeleton' laws[1] about 'the general legal status of the press and of films'. In 1948–49, most of the eleven *Länder* of the German federation had passed press laws of varying scope and which contained divergent regulations. The German Federal Government later introduced a press 'frame' bill in March 1952 which was intended to achieve a national consistency in press regulations. An extensive bill, containing sixty-four paragraphs, it certainly contained the demanded recognition by the press of its public duty and conceded the maintenance of legitimate press interests in the sense of paragraph 193 of the German Legal Code. But it still aroused the fervent opposition of the German press organizations.

Press opposition to the bill was catalysed by several restrictions that it would place upon the press's freedom, i.e.: protecting the image of the German federation and its democratic order; the peaceful co-existence of nations; respect for the morals; religion and person of others; and an obligation to truth. These seemingly positive restrictions in the bill were couched in partially elastic terms which, when coupled with its strict regulations and penalties, would allow for the growth of extensive government interference in the press.

At the centre of the press's attack on the bill was a clause which provided for both federal and state press committees comprised of two judges from the respective courts and four representatives each from both the publishers' and journalists' organizations.

The press was particularly offended that committee members were to have been named by the appropriate governments in office. In that, the press saw an enforced self-control with vast potential for governmental interference and influence. The bill finally died because of the opposition of the press. However, journalists also regretted its death in part because some provisions of the bill provided for the detailed regulation of the publisher-editor relationship in accordance with the goals of the journalist's organizations.

During the era following 1952, the federation made no further attempts to pass 'frame' law, and discussion about such a law has only been resumed since 1969.

1. See footnote 2, page 17.

A law enacted in the autumn of 1952 concerning the circulation of works endangering minors renewed extreme arguments and protests from the press, mainly from the publishers. This law serves to protect minors from morally endangering publications. To that end, the law authorized the establishment of a Federal Examining Authority which has the right to indicate which publications endanger the public morals. Works so indicated may not be then offered for public sale.

Since 1953, the communication policies of the German federation have shifted away from the overt regulation of specific areas as applied to the press to a covert area of general law not openly specified for the press.

This trend could be seen as early as 1952, when the federation enacted a new industrial relations law (*Betriebsverfassungsgesetz*). Over the union resistance which it provoked, this act restricts management participation by unionship counsel within so-called 'trend' businesses which are so defined as to include publishing houses. A new 1971 version of this law retained this regulation despite journalists joining in the protest against it.

A 1953 revision of paragraph 53 of the German Penal Code brought about an extension of the existing press 'shield' law. But, it was viewed as insufficient by professional organizations, and no subsequent changes have been made in it despite press pressure. However the press has been able to put its conceptions through in *Länder* press laws passed between 1964 and 1966.

Despite those gains on the State level, the press's drive to revise paragraph 353-C of the German Legal Code remains unsuccessful. This section threatens legal punishment for the communication of State secrets, even by members of the press. This regulation was again discussed by the Bundestag in 1972, but was retained in force.

Since 1953, repeated attempts by the federal government to co-ordinate the public information activities of the federal ministries by organizational means have similarly foundered. The same is true of its attempts to create a Ministry of Information as an instrument for propagating the government's policies.

It was more successful with a 1957 amendment to the Penal Code which prohibits untrue or grossly distorted allegations about the Bundeswehr.[1] Despite the press's opposition to these 'muzzle' paragraphs, the amendment was put into effect.

A development similar to the press 'shield' problem arose in the question of impounding a publisher's property for publishing illegal and punishable material. In 1955, the parliamentary fraction of the SPD presented a bill to liberalize the corresponding regulations in the Code of Criminal Procedure, and the federal government responded by presenting its own bill a year later. The latter aroused the press's objections because it largely failed to fulfil their expectations.

In 1953, the federal government presented the draft of a broadcasting bill

---

1. *Bundeswehr* is literally translated as the Federal Defence Force, and is used to designate the three branches of the German federation's armed services.

that was intended to extend its broadcasting authority previously restricted by direction of the occupying powers. It was never enacted due to the resistance of the *Länder* which did not want the federal government to trim any of their own broadcasting authority excepting that of telecommunications engineering. The ensuing discussion between the federation and the *Länder* about a treaty to solve the problem was also inconclusive. Failure greeted yet another attempt by the federal government in 1959. The bill it presented at that time provided for the establishment of a federal broadcasting system for the domestic broadcasting of German-language radio programmes and for representing the Federal Republic's interests abroad: Deutschlandfunk (German Radio) and Deutsche Welle (German Wave). It also provided for establishing a nationwide Television Germany that would be under the extensive influence of the federal government.

The latter part of the bill also provided for the participation of private companies as programming sources for the television channel. It was not only protested by the parliamentary opposition, the unions and the churches, but by the member *Länder* above all. Due to the states' opposition, the Bundesrat (Federal Council) was not expected to give its required approval. The federal government subsequently entered into new negotiations with the *Länder*. A compromise agreement was almost reached when Chancellor Adenauer surprisingly moved to found a German Television Incorporated with the Federal Minister of Justice acting as trustee for the *Länder*. A few of the *Länder* thereupon filed suit before the Federal Constitutional Court. The so-called 'Television Judgement' that it passed down in 1961 declared the plans of the federal government to be unconstitutional. In its stead, the *Länder* founded the second German television (ZDF) in June of 1961 by an interstate treaty.

An attempt by the federation to legally extend the 'personal protection law' (libel and slander codes) was equally unsuccessful, especially in respect as to how it was reported in the press. The federal government made a further attempt to strengthen the libel codes under criminal law as applied to foreign heads of State. It failed passage in the summer of 1968, and the Federal Ministry of Justice thereupon presented the draft of a bill for re-regulating the civil libel and slander codes. The press principally rejected the stipulations about the right of injured parties to damage claims and advanced an anchoring of the press's 'public duty' in law. It is true that a bill for the latter was thereupon introduced, but the press associations remained adament. The whole libel code project was finally dropped by all parties.

The federal government could not realize its conceptions about press restrictions even in the passage of emergency powers laws. The first emergency powers bill was presented in 1960. It would have given the government the emergency power to restrict the press in restoring order. The draft was defeated by the resistance of both the Bundesrat (Federal Council) and the parliamentary opposition. In 1962, the federal cabinet issued a second bill which differentiated between foreign and domestic emergencies but which still irritated the press. It provided for press restrictions in both cases and thus collided with the resistance of a press that would tolerate no such restrictions in the case of foreign emergencies. In addition, the press demanded that an organization be established in which it should be extensively included to advise and control the press in domestic emergencies. The resulting efforts to reach a compromise draft came to naught, because the press and the government could not agree on the composition of such an emergency press commission. The emergency powers laws which were finally enacted in 1968 contained no such restrictions on Article 5 of the 1949 constitution.

The press achieved further success in an amendment to the Penal Code enacted at about the same time. Discussion over this amendment arose in 1962 as the German magazine *Der Spiegel* was subjected to extensive impoundment and seizure as a result of an allegedly treasonous article that it published. The long-standing discussion about reforming the political legal code finally brought on amendments to the Legal Code which fulfilled the press's expectations. Above all, the amendment differentiates between 'normal' and 'journalistic' State treason.

Meanwhile, the complaints of the newspaper publishers about broadcasting competition for advertising had reached a high pitch. The publishers were particularly concerned about the economic dangers posed to the press by rising broadcast advertising. In early 1964, they published an extensive memorandum on the subject. A few months later, the Federal Parliament charged the goverment to institute an independent commission of experts. Named after its chairman, the Michel Commission was to examine the competetive relationship between the press, broadcasting and film industries. Its findings were presented in 1967 and contradicted the claims made by the publishers' memorandum. The commission especially rejected the publishers' demands to be included in broadcasting operations as that would lead to the development of undesirable multimedia monopolies. The federal government largely concurred with the commission's report.

It was also at about this time that a bill presented by the Christlich Soziale Union (CSU)/Christlich Demokratische Union (CDU) and FDP government fractions in parliament was not enacted. It would have forbidden advertising by public broadcasting. The bill collapsed against the resistance of the SPD opposition in parliament which had been against private broadcasting from the beginning, and against the *Länder*'s resistance as they wanted to protect their own public broadcasters' rights to carry advertising.

A series of spectacular magazine mergers in the mid-sixties brought the problems of press concentration back to the centre of media policy discussion. The federal government was so aroused by the mergers that it instituted a commission of inquiry in 1967. The Guenther Commission, named after its chairman, was different from the Michel Commission in that it was made up of representatives from the affected press organizations, broadcasting and the general public. After a few months, the Guenther Commission presented a catalogue of recommendations which summoned the press to restrict its competition, and advanced a series of financial aid measures such as credit, tax relief and reduced postage fees. The federal government partially concurred and granted the financially weaker newspaper publishers a sales tax reimbursement and credit from European Recovery Programme funds.

The Guenther Commission aroused more controversy with the recommendations made in its final report in 1968. Next to financial aid, the report urged that press concentration be countered by placing upper limits on any one publisher's market share, and by supporting newspapers instituted as counter weights to existing monopolies.

The federal government finally took over the commission's recommendations for financial aid, for improving the situation of journalists, for carefully observing business developments of the press, for urging more transparency in the publishers' property reports, and for establishing a board of trustees for newspaper management and technology.

In July 1969, the Bundestag called upon the federal government to issue regular reports about the state of the media, to aid in enacting merger control laws, and to re-examine both free market laws and the state of journalists' social security. It also urged the legal regulation of publishers' stock and property reports. The government reacted to the first of the requests by issuing an *Intermediate Report* on the media in April 1970. In the autumn of 1969, the government additionally announced that the other requests made by the Bundestag would be met and that a press 'skeleton' law would be enacted. These proposals have been further discussed and prepared for, but have not been met as of 1973. The same is true of the press statistic law announced by the federal government in its 1970 *Intermediate Report*.

3.2 The communication policies of the *Länder* of the German Federal Republic, 1948—72

With the approval of the occupying powers, the *Länder* of the present Federal Republic began taking communication policy initiatives even before the era of allied press licencing was over. In 1948, the broadcasting institutes of the *Länder* were created by state laws or through interstate treaties. The same year saw the *Länder* beginning to pass press laws which were still bound to certain allied prescriptions. Thus, the *Länder* in the United States Zone (Bremen, Hessen, Baden-Württemberg and Bavaria) enacted press laws modelled after the 1874 press laws of the German Empire. The three *Länder* in the British Zone (Schleswig-Holstein, Hamburg and Nordrhein-Westfalen) issued partial regulations for the press which were mainly concerned with establishing professional stipulations for journalists and publishers, and which also provided for the creation of press advisory committees. These committees had to advise the respective *Länder* governments on all matters concerning the press and to participate in any professional ban proceedings against members of the press. However, there have been no professional bans since 1959 when the Federal Constitutional Court declared the corresponding stipulations in the Nordrhein-Westfalen press law to be unconstitutional.

Following that judgement, the *Länder* issued regulations relevent to the media, but which were contained in the framework of general laws. These are too numerous to be treated in this publication, but one good example of these should be mentioned: the *Land* of Hessen enacted an amendment to its impoundment law in 1958. It resulted from an action against newspapers which carried controversial election advertising during the 1957 elections and were therefore impounded. The Hessian amendment was a product of close co-operation between the state ministries, experts on press law and representatives of the press. It clearly improved the position of the press in such questions, and, for the first time, provided for damage payments for improper and unjustified impoundment. Thus, it was to serve the press organizations as a model for corresponding provisions lobbied for in press laws later enacted by the other *Länder*.

Schleswig-Holstein was the first *Land* to initiate the revision of *Land* press laws. In the summer of 1959, the minister-president of Schleswig-Holstein asked the German Press Council to develop conceptions for such a law and to pass those on to the ministers-president of all the German *Länder*. On the basis of those recommendations, a 1960 conference of the *Länder*'s interior ministers agreed to a model *Land* press law draft. It was generally approved by the press, although not in all detail. But, due to an alternative draft presented by Nordrhein-Westfalen and the reservations of the *Länder's* departments of justice, the draft was revised. In February 1963, the Conference of Interior Ministers approved a draft that was clearly more conservative than the first.

The purpose of the model draft was to standardize the press laws of the *Länder*, but that purpose was only conditionally fulfilled. Due to the objections and demands of the press, the formulations of the model draft were extensively altered in a few of the *Länder* to favour the press. The results of state press legislation which ended in 1966 are uniform in their construction and extent, but differ as to the detailed regulations. The resultant press laws generally contain most of the press's recommendations. The press was especially successful in having its 'public duty' officially recognized by these laws, and in achieving friendly regulation of information access law, 'shield' law, impoundment law and 'fairness' law. By the end of 1966, all states except Bavaria and Hessen had revised their press laws. However, Hessen had modernized its 1949 press law by an extensive series of amendments.

In broadcasting, one finds that the North-west German Broadcasting System (NWDR) was divided in the mid-fifties into the North German and West German Broadcasting Systems (NDR and WDR). This effected a breakthrough of the general construction principles for state broadcasting that had been in effect until then. Both the 1955 interstate treaty establishing the NDR and the 1954 *Land* broadcasting law establishing the WDR provided that the construction of their broadcasting councils correspond to the party representation in the respective *Länder* parliaments. They thus abandoned the current principle of a council made up of various social groups which had been established in the other *Länder*.

The *Länder* were also successful in a conflict with the federal government over broadcasting authority which had begun in the early fifties. Because the

'Television Judgement' handed down by the Federal Constitutional Court in February of 1961 confirmed the *Länder*'s claim to that authority, they signed an interstate treaty in June of the same year to establish the second German television network (ZDF).

A year later, the ministers-president of the *Länder* agreed to restrict broadcast advertising to counter the danger of its overexpansion. The amount of daily advertising is limited to twenty minutes per channel, and it may not be broadcast on Sundays, holidays, or after eight o'clock in the evening.

Although the *Länder* have extensively relinquished their media authority over the question of press concentration to the federal government, they have been deploying a certain activity in the development of broadcasting policies. Thus, during the television conflict with the federal government, many *Land* governments were trying to determine if there was a distortion of advertising competition between public broadcasting and the press. They were also concerned with the problem of private broadcasting. As of yet, no *Land* has granted private broadcasting concessions; the reason being the lack of suitable legal regulations in almost all of the *Länder*. The licensing of private broadcasting is theoretically possible in Schleswig-Holstein. And, in Berlin, a legal battle developed between a publishers' association interested in broadcasting and the *Land* government. In 1971, the highest authority, the Federal Administrative Court, decided against the publishers.

Finally, in 1967, Saarland enacted an amendment to its broadcasting law which allows the licensing of private broadcasters. However, there is an ongoing legal dispute about both its realization and content. This, and the lack of a free channel, have, up to now, hindered the concessioning of a private station although there is no lack of interested parties.

The *Land* of Hessen took a unique path in defusing the problem of advertising competition between public broadcasting and the private press. In 1963, the minister-president of Hessen arranged an agreement between the Hessian Broadcasting System and the Hessian Association of Newspaper Publishers which aimed at co-ordinating their respective interests regarding broadcast advertising.

In 1965, the ministers-president of the *Länder* rejected a proposal made by the Federal Association of German Newpaper Publishers for taking over programme production for the ZDF by a publishers' production company. Apart from the juridical problems arising from the organizational and public construction of the ZDF network, this recommendation also contradicted communication policy recommendations such as the Michel Commission report.

In 1968, the *Länder* of Baden-Württemberg, Rheinland-Pfalz and the Saarland instituted a commission of experts to develop recommendations for a more purposeful broadcasting structure in the south-west region as three different broadcasting systems exist in that area: Saarlaendischer Rundfunk (Saarland Broadcasting System), Suedwestfunk (South-west Broadcasting) and the Sueddeutscher Rundfunk (South German Broadcasting). Saarlaendischer

Rundfunk has only a very small fee collecting area,[1] Suedwestfunk has no geographically closed fee collecting area, and the *Land* of Baden-Wuerttemberg is the only *Land* divided between two broadcasting system fee collecting areas: Suedwestfunk and Sueddeutscher Rundfunk.

The commission could not agree on any particular solutions. A small majority favoured the creation of a broadcasting system for Baden-Wuerttemberg and a single system for Saarland and Rheinland-Pfalz. No agreement was reached because the *Länder* involved have differing concepts about a solution. The problem has been set aside in favour of closer co-operation between the three systems in south-west Germany. This delay is also closely related to the problem of a re-apportionment of the *Länder* which has not yet been accomplished. Any action to be taken on the corresponding reorganization of the respective broadcasting systems is awaiting that re-apportionment.

There have lately been efforts by the *Länder* to expand their press laws so as to include regulation of publishers' stock and property statements. These efforts are intended to bring more transparency to the press and thus enable the reader to form an accurate picture of the respective paper's ownership.

The *Länder*'s press laws of 1948–49 had already contained such provisions, but they were so ill defined that they proved to be of little effect and were not carried over into subsequent press laws. In the light of the findings of the Guenther Commission which were thoroughly endorsed by the federal government, the *Länder* were motivated to co-operate with the German Press Council in discussing appropriate property report regulations while considering past experience. However, one *Land*, Bavaria, had already introduced effective regulations of publisher stock and property statements in 1950.

3.3 Government measures for the advancement of film in the Federal Republic of Germany

FEDERAL AND 'LAND' SPONSORSHIP

In 1946, the Allied Powers began distributing licences for film production to west German film producers. That licensing was abolished upon the introduction of the Federal Republic's constitution in 1949. That same year saw the number of west German feature productions rise to sixty-two.

An excess of older, amortized films from the United States and from Ufa[2] archives depressed prices and subsequently reduced the profit chances of new film productions on the west German market. Hard times fell upon many an undercapitalized, small and divided west German production company.

---

1. Public broadcasting in the Federal Republic of Germany is primarily financed by the levying of legally mandatory fees on the viewers and listeners.
2. Ufa stands for Universum Film AG, a private company founded in 1917. When the Nazis consolidated the entire German film industry in 1942, they used the Ufa name to designate the parent film company. In post-war west Germany this corporation was split up, and returned to private hands. A private Ufa company was re-established in 1953.

Ailing studios existed in the *Länder* of Berlin, Hamburg, Niedersachsen, Bavaria and Hessen. Beginning in 1949, these *Länder* took steps to help their ailing studios by guaranteeing indemnity to banks holding loans on film productions. That meant that any lenders' deficits would be fully covered by the *Länder*. Soon afterwards the federal government experimented with the same policy for a while. This indemnity action has been a losing proposition for the *Länder*. Bavaria alone has lost over DM.20 million through this policy.

The federal government first took steps to provide film security in an enactment that went into effect on 31 March 1950 and which ended on 31 March 1953, providing DM.22 million for production indemnities.

This sum supported eighty-two feature films and feature length cultural films during that period.

Conditions for securing indemnity were the prior examination of the script and subsequent production supervision by the German Audit and Trust Co. Losses from this first film indemnity action totalled DM.8.1 million.

A second federal indemnity action went into effect in the autumn of 1953, and was subsidized with a sum of DM.78 million. Seventy-six films received security; and total losses to the federal government from this action are currently over DM.23.1 million. The government halted this badly losing proposition in 1955.

FILM PREMIUMS AND PRIZES AWARDED BY THE FEDERAL MINISTRY OF THE INTERIOR

After 1955, all federal measures for film support were restricted to the awarding of prizes and premiums through the auspices of the Federal Ministry of the Interior. These were first distributed in 1951. In 1956, after the suspension of federal film indemnities, the prizes and awards were increased considerably. And, in 1968, they were again revised upwards. The awards are as follows:

Federal film prizes. Feature films: Gold Cup, DM.500,000; Filmstrip in Gold, DM.400,000; Filmstrip in Silver, DM.350.000. Cultural and documentary films: Filmstrip in Gold, DM.120,000; Filmstrip in Silver, DM.100,000. Short films: Filmstrip in Gold, DM.40,000; Filmstrip in Silver, DM.30,000.

Feature-length premiums. This premium for the support of 'good feature-length films' amounts to DM.250,000 or DM.200,000.

Cultural film premiums. Feature-length films: Black and white, DM.60,000; colour, DM.80,000. Short films: Black and white, DM.15,000; colour, DM.20,000.

Film script premiums (film project premiums). Qualitatively distinguished feature film projects may be supported by a premium of DM.200,000, with another DM.10,000 going to the screenwriter. The amount may be raised to DM.300,000 for new film makers. Short film projects may receive a premium amounting to 40 per cent of the projected costs.

All of the prizes and premiums are conditionally awarded. That means they must be used for the production of new films.

FILM ADVANCEMENT BY THE KURATORIUM JUNGER DEUTSCHER FILM

In the 'Oberhausener Manifest' of 1962, twenty-six film directors and screen-writers put forward the claim 'to make new German feature films'. As a result of their initiative, the Federal Ministry of the Interior was enabled by an enactment passed in 1964 to establish the Kuratorium Junger Deutscher Film (Board for Current German Films) in Munich on 1 February 1965. The board was originally financed by the Federal Ministry of the Interior with a fund of approximately DM.5 million from 1966 to 1969. Between 1966 and 1968 twenty film projects were supported. This sum was used for loans to young German directors in financing their first feature films. If the films were successful, the loans were repaid and profits were to be divided with the board. These sums were to have flowed back into a fund administered by the board. However, the fund was quickly depleted as the commercial success of the films fell far below expectations.

Since 1969, the German *Länder* have taken over support of the trust fund by a yearly endowment of DM.750,000. Therewith the first film projects of young German directors would be supported with loans of up to DM.250,000. In 1971 the board has ceased to support production exclusively and now supports distribution as well. Distribution of any one film can be supported by up to DM.60,000, 50 per cent of which is to be used for making copies and 50 per cent of which is to go to the Bureau for Film Co-ordination which organizes distribution. Next to that, the board supports film theatres which contract to show films supported by the board.

SUPPORT OF FILMS THROUGH THE LAW FOR THE ADVANCEMENT OF FILM

On 22 December 1967 the Federal Parliament enacted a law for Measures for the Advancement of German Film (*Filmfoerderungsgesetz*), and it revised the law on 9 August 1971. The law's essential conditions are as follows.

A public institute, the Filmförderungsanstalt (Film Advancement Institute), was created in Berlin for the subsidizing of native German films. The institute is supervised by the Minister of Economics. It has the duties of supporting films by raising the over-all quality of German films, subsidizing German-foreign co-productions, advising the federal government on film policy (especially with regard to the European Economic Community (EEC)), cultivating co-operation between television and the film industry, and working for efficiency in distribution.

The institute guarantees help to producers for the production of native films or international co-productions, to theatre-owners for renewal and improvements of the technical projection and interior decorations, and to agencies which carry out both domestic and foreign advertising for German films. This is all funded by a special fee levied on all commercial screenings in the Federal Republic and West Berlin. This fee amounts to 10 pfennigs (DM.0.10) charged on each ticket to a feature film and a 5 pfennigs surcharge on short films or childrens' shows.

The funds raised by the fee, approximately DM.15 million in 1972, are redistributed to film producers. If a subsidizable film earns within twenty-four months a gross distribution revenue of DM.500,000 or DM. 300,000 if it has received a predicate from the Film Evaluation Bureau (FBW), it will receive a subsidy determined according to available funds and the number of films to be supported. The average base sum in 1972 was DM.250,000. An additional sum of DM.250,000 maximum is awarded if a film has either received a predicate from the FBW, been designated as a 'good entertainment film' by the 'small commission' of the institute, or if it had won a top prize at an 'A festival'. Additional funds can be given to such films even if it had only netted a gross distribution revenue of DM.100,000 at the time of the award. A 'poor-quality clause' prevents subsidies being awarded to poor-grade films such as commercial pornography.

The federal law for the advancement of film is primarily concerned with the economic aspects of the film industry as the German constitution delegates cultural authority to the member *Länder* and the federal government has only non-specific film authority. Only the most important film support measures have been described here. Further federal and *Länder* measures as well as community measures cannot be described in detail in the space available.

4 Communication policies of the private media institutes

Most of the communication policies of the private media institutes are related either to the communication policies of the *Länder* and the federation or occur within the frame of the professional organizations and are therefore described in Chapters 3 and 5. It is intended that only the question of self-control will be additionally touched upon in the outline required here.

Since the first post-war years, different recommendations have been made for institutionalizing a self-control of the media, especially in the press. Only a few these recommendations ever became reality.[1]

4.1 The self-control of illustrated magazines

The Selbskontrolle Illustrierter Zeitschriften (SIZ) (Self-control of Illustrated Magazines) represents an attempt at self-control which had different but hardly effective predecessors since 1949. Its immediate predecessor was the Self-control of German Illustrateds (SDI) which was founded in 1957. It was comprised of a working group of the publishers and editors-in-chief (of the participating magazines) and a co-council with representatives from the churches as well as from family, youth and educational organizations. In 1964, the co-council ceased its operation because it had essentially only an advisory function, because it felt that the participating magazines were not adhering to the guidelines, and because it no longer wanted to function as an 'alibi'.

In 1966, the SIZ was founded. 'Personalities of public life' were, in fact, given a vote, however, they were still a minority to a majority of representatives from the publishers and editorial staffs. After different magazines joined and left the organizations with regularity, the magazine publishers withdrew entirely from the SIZ in 1971. Its last chairman, the Reverend Eberhard

---

1. An extensive description for the area of the press is to be found in Rolf Richter, *Kommunikationsfreiheit = Verlegerfreiheit? Zur Kommunikationspolitik der Zeitungsverleger in der Bundesrepublik Deutschland 1945-1969* [Communications Freedom = Publisher Freedom? Communication Policies of the Newspaper Publishers in the Federal Republic of Germany, 1945-1969], p. 271 et seq., Pullach bei München, 1973. (Dortmunder Beiträge zur Zeitungsforschung, Vol. 17.)

Stammler, thereupon gave the following comments about the final suspension of SIZ:[1]

After the magazine publishers which supported the SIZ withdrew from it, a further functioning of this institution has become impossible. Under these conditions, the chairman and the professionally competent members have been forced to recognize ... that the SIZ no longer exists. They regret this development, because, as a voluntary association, the charter of the SIZ gave it the duty to be concerned 'that the illustrated magazine publishers, as a part of the free press, take their responsibilities to society seriously'. In a democratic State such responsibilities can be best authenticated in the form of self-control. That this could not be carried out in the illustrated magazine branch is a serious appearance in a democratic society.

Against that, the Association of German Magazine Publishers (VDZ) characterized the dissolution of the SIZ as a 'directly necessary last step because its work has been ineffective, not just recently, but since years. . . . The function of the SIZ and beyond that, the maintenance of all the free press' social responsibility has been long since successfully taken over by the German Press Council with extensively large success, and is even anchored in its standing orders'.

4.2 The German Press Council

As with the other self-control organs of the private media, the Deutsche Presserat (German Press Council) was primarily founded with a view towards avoiding feared State measures, especially legislative and executive actions. After immediate post-war attempts to legally enact the creation of press committees or similar self-control organs, the Hamburg Journalists' Association in the German Journalists Association (DJV) developed plans for voluntary self-control. Despite initial hesitation on the part of the newspaper publishers, the DJV and the Federal Association of German Newspaper Publishers (EDZV) finally agreed to found the German Press Council in 1956, which was joined a year later by the Association of German Magazine Publishers (VDZ) as the organization of magazine publishers.

The Press Council comprises two groups of ten representatives each from the publishers and the journalists, and which may elect five 'further personalities from the press'. According to its statutes, from 1 January 1959, the council has the following duties: '(a) to protect the freedom of the press, to ensure free and unhindered access to news sources; (b) to confirm abuses in the press and to correct them; (c) to observe structural developments in the German press and to resist concern and monopoly developments which endanger freedom; (d) to represent the German press to government, parliament and the public, especially in legislative bills which affect the life and duties of the press.'

1. cf. *Sueddeutsche Zeitung*, No. 168, 15 July, 1971, p. 6 and *ZV + ZV*, No. 30–31, 1971, p. 1378.

The statutes further provide that the Press Council convene, 'as the occasion demands, but regularly every three months', in a closed session. It may make its most important decisions public, and is to present annually a public report of its activities.[1]

Although the Press Council has absolutely no executive authority, its effectiveness is generally more positively judged than that of the other media organs of self-control. That the council is unlike comparable foreign institutions, in that it can be both called into session by anyone or act upon its own initiative, gains it favourable judgement. However, even the German Press Council has not been spared criticism. It has had its main success in repelling State measures against the press and in co-operating in legislative planning, while it has been shown to be less effective in 'internal' matters, that is, in its own control of the press. Thus, it has all too easily come to be viewed as being less friendly to publicity about internal matters than about its actions repelling State interference. It has also been adversely criticized because the Press Council does not, in principle, convene in public, an action which could raise its stature, authority and effectiveness.

In the last few years, the German Press Council has also intensively taken up the problem of journalists' training and education, a problem which is increasingly becoming a factor in communication policy initiatives.

4.3 The voluntary self-control of the film industry

The Freiwillige Selbstkontrolle der Filmwirtschaft (FSK) (Voluntary Self-control of the Film Industry) was founded as a section of the Leading Organization of the Film Industry (SPIO) in 1949 and therewith replaced the occupying powers' film censorship with mandatory approval procedures for all films to be publicly shown.

The FSK decides if a film: (a) will be approved for showing at all, or else; (b) from which age the film may be shown (from 6, 12, 16 or 18 years); (c) if it may be shown on Sundays and holidays.

According to the guidelines of the FSK established on 17 March 1955, 'no films should be produced, distributed, or publicity shown which are likely to damage moral or religious sensibilities, promote anti-democratic, militaristic, imperialistic, nationalistic or racist tendencies, endanger the relationships between Germany and other States, demean constitutional principles, or falsify historical facts'.[2]

---

1. The statutes are included in the *Tätigkeitsbericht 1970* (1970 annual report of the German Press Council), p. 124-6. Bonn–Bad Godesberg, 1971.
2. Elisabeth Noelle-Neumann and Winfried Schulz (eds.), *Fischer Lexikon Publizistik*, op. cit., p. 315.

Until 1971, each film had to undergo an examination by the FSK at its own expense before it was publicity shown. This was based upon an obligation of all the members of the SPIO branch associations not to distribute or show films which were not approved by the FSK. The binding obligations of the FSK judgements on the films of non-SPIO members were secured through corresponding declarations recognizing the FSK's authority.

The FSK comprises three authorities: the controlling authority is the working committee which steer two convening authorities, the main committee and the legal committee. In these, the federal government, *Länder*, churches, and the Bundesjugendring (Federal Youth Association) are represented along with the film industry. Unlike the SIZ and the German Press Council, the FSK has executive authority: it can issue warnings and reprimands, stop delivery and acceptance, and impose fines.

The creation of this voluntary self-control of the film industry served the purpose of avoiding State censorship as was specifically provided for in the Weimar Constitution and through the Reichslichtspiel (Film) law of 1920, changed and strengthened in 1934, which regulated it, and which was practised by the allied powers in the immediate years after 1945. Although it is not clearly explained in constitutional law if the examinations of the FSK conflict with the censorship ban in Article 5 of the constitution, and although they have only a partial and indirect legal basis, the FSK worked essentially unchanged until 1971 and thus fulfilled its most important function of protecting the high capital investments in the film industry from State interference.

The FSK concentrated its activities on film sexuality and brutality. However, competition, mainly from television, forced the industry to 'specialize' in these restricted areas. This led to a strengthening of the FSK's activities in the 1960s: the yearly average of films designated as 'adult', with entrance restricted to those over 18, was 21 per cent of all examined films between 1959 and 1963. This proportion rose to 45 per cent in 1969. At the same time, the 'semi-official censorship practice' of the FSK was being increasingly questioned by such developments as the expansion of publicly accepted borders of toleration in sexual areas, the increasing ignoring of the FSK's injunctions, and television which is not under the control of the FSK and which increasingly broadcast 'unexamined' films. It must remain unexplained here, as to what extent this development was contributed to by the pressure of those film industry interests which saw, and still see, their future as primarily or exclusively in sex films.

In 1971, this led the church representatives to withdraw from the FSK out of protest against their 'alibi function', and to a reform of the FSK shortly thereafter.

The new guidelines provide that the previous examination methods with the participation of the State, the churches and the Federal Youth Association would be restricted to the protection of minors and to the question of whether a film may be shown on Sundays and holidays.

However, the decision to permit the showing of an 'adult' film according to FSK standards now rests exclusively with delegates called up by the film industry, but who are not allowed to be active in it themselves. Moreover, this control can be selectively replaced by a purely legal examination by the legal board of the SPIC which can certify that a film merits an X-rating of not being 'punishably offensive'.[1]

1. cf. Horst von Hartlieb, 'Filmrecht', in Emil Dovifat (ed.), *Handbuch der Publizistik*, Vol. 2, Part 1, p. 218-19; Koszyk and Pruys, op. cit., p. 127; *Der Spiegel*, No. 10, 1972, p. 145-6; Noelle-Neumann and Schulz (eds.), op. cit., p. 26, 34 and 314-15.

5 Communication policies of professional organizations of the media

5.1 The Federal Association of German Newspaper Publishers

The Bundesverband Deutscher Zeitungsverleger e.V. (BDZV) (Federal Association of German Newspaper Publishers) was formed in 1952 as a result of the merger between the Joint League of German Newspaper Publishers (GDZV) and the Association of German Newspaper Publishers (VDZV).[1] With close to 500 members, the new association includes almost every newspaper publisher in the Federal Republic of Germany.

Conflicts arose in the years before the merger between the two associations. They were over press legalities, but had their origin in the competitive situation between the publishers' groups. Thus, post-war north German publishers who were licensed by the Allies had attempted to establish legally detailed conditions for both the publishing trade and press control committees. The pre-war publishers were not totally unjustified in rejecting these attempts as instruments of warding off their competition. However, they could not prevent the inclusion of similar provisions in the press laws passed by three north German *Länder* in 1949. As it was, these provisions had little effect. In 1959, the German Constitutional Court declared them to be unconstitutional.

A 1952 attempt by the German federal government to establish similar committees[2] by a press bill likewise foundered. That bill's intended committee was to have discussed all aspects of the press, to have insured both its independence and loyalty, and to have observed concentration tendencies in the publishing area. The BDZV and other press organizations rejected the committee concept because they feared government interference in their free operations. Following that, the idea of a legislated press committee was dropped.[3] *Länder* laws passed in 1964–66 no longer contained such regulations. In its stead, the press founded the German Press Council in 1956 as a voluntary organ of self-control.[4]

In the mid-fifties, publishers shifted their attention to broadcasting. If they had only vaguely discussed the possibilities of commercial radio and had

---

1. The Allies had prohibited all pre-war, Nazi-era, publishers from continuing in their trade.
2. The proposed committees were to have comprised representatives from the press organizations and the general public.
3. Discussion about legislated press boards has only recently been resumed: see Section 7.1.
4. Compare this to the DJV proposals discussed later in Section 4 of this chapter.

hardly criticized advertising carried by public radio, they took the advent of television much more seriously. Thus, two goals crystallized in their broadcasting policies: (a) to have all advertising carried by public broadcasting banned; (b) to have publisher participation in a private broadcasting system.

A suit brought by the BDZV to have public broadcasting advertising banned as both illegal and uncompetitive was lost in 1957. After that, the BDZV then concentrated on gaining participation in a second television network that was being planned at the time. During its preparations, however, a conflict over administrative authority arose between the *Land* and federal governments and which was only resolved in 1961 by the so-called 'television judgement' of the German Constitutional Court. This judgement gave exclusive broadcasting authority to the *Länder*, declared a federally sponsored Television Germany to be unconstitutional,[1] and dissolved a private broadcasting corporation that had been meanwhile founded by some publishers. Shortly afterwards, the German *Länder* contracted among themselves to establish a second German television network (ZDF) which is likewise a public system. The BDZV then shifted the gravity of its broadcasting policies towards the removal of the 'competition distortions' which the publishers saw as existing between public broadcasting, with both its secure fee basis and rising advertising on the one hand, and the private press on the other. In 1964, the BDZV circulated a memorandum accusing the public broadcasting institutes of being 'almost governmental' and which predicted the decline of the free press if no action were to be taken against the 'competition distortions'. That memorandum provoked the federal government into appointing an independent examining commission.[2] Its findings were published in 1967, and not only rejected the contentions of the memorandum but opposed any publisher-operated television because of related monopoly dangers.

Other attempts to establish a publishers' television had collapsed in the meanwhile; a plan developed by the publishers in 1964 to take over the programming of ZDF was rejected by the *Länder*. The Federal Parliament shortly thereafter failed to pass a bill which would have banned the carrying of advertising by public broadcasters and would have indirectly established a basis for private broadcasting.

At present, the only explicit legal basis for establishment of private broadcasting exists in Saarland where the broadcasting law was amended in 1967 to allow for it. But, because no frequencies were available, the government of Saarland has granted no concessions to the holding company, partially owned by publishers, which was formed as a result of the amendment. Moreover, the Saarland broadcasting law is legally contested.

Many publishers had already dropped the idea of private broadcasting because of rising installation costs and falling advertising profits. Many financially weaker publishers had aspired all along less to broadcasting than

1. The court based its judgement on the fact that the constitutionally guaranteed independence of broadcasting from the State was not sufficiently guaranteed by Television Germany.
2. The Michel Commission which has been discussed previously on page 24.

to working out an arrangement with the broadcasters to demarcate their respective spheres of interest and bring about extensive co-operation regarding, above all, the extent and pricing of broadcast advertising. At the moment, such arrangements have only been reached in Hessen.

The present position of the BDZV on broadcasting is easily summed up: it is against the establisment of localized broadcasting. If such local broadcasting stations were to be established, then the publishers argue that they should be proportionally included in the operations as they would be the first affected by the loss of local advertising revenues to them.

Next to the question of 'inner' freedom of the press,[1] press concentration has clearly emerged as a major problem since the mid-sixties. It is true that the concentration had already begun and was steadily advancing in the fifties, but it was either hardly noticed, or, as in the case of the publishers, trifled over. Serious discussion about this problem began only after extensive mergers in the illustrated magazine branch stirred public notice. It thereafter became clear that even the seemingly high number of 1,500 news publications in 1954 were produced by only 225 'complete' news staffs. By 1963 this number had sunk to 190 and stands today at about 130 (1973). In addition to that, there are newspaper monopolies in almost a third of the cities and counties in the Federal Republic of Germany.

In 1967, a Press Commission or Guenther Commission was appointed to examine this development and its effects on the freedom of communication. The commission was composed of representatives from the press, public broadcasting and from the general public. Some months later, it quickly presented a catalogue of recommendations for immediate action. It took over, almost word for word, the publishers' recommendations for tax relief and inexpensive credit for the press. But the commission's final report went further to recommend that the market proportions of any one publisher be limited, that local competition be advanced to establish market balances, and that the smaller publishers be supported.

These incitements were reproached as unconstitutional by the publishers' association and a few commission members as well. The association apparently wanted an across-the-board financial relief for all publishers regardless of their size, and not any purposeful policies for shaping press structure in the Federal Republic of Germany. But the BDZV was split on these recommendations for there was much in their structural policies that the financially weaker publishers could agree with. The federal government only took up the commission's recommendations for a yearly structure report, for legally requiring property and stock reports by the publishers, and for the establishment of competitive rules and a board of newspaper technology and business. It had already guaranteed credit and tax relief for small publishers in 1967.

1. What is here meant is the publisher–editor relationship; compare this to the positions discussed in the following paragraphs.

5.2 **The Association of German Magazine Publishers**

In 1949 the Verband Deutscher Zeitschriftenverleger e.V. (VDZ) (Association of German Magazine Publishers) was formed out of the Pool of German Magazine Publishers Associations. But it did not consider itself as having any employer's bargaining powers. It is something like the BDZV as it is a parent organization of regional publishers associations.

The effective policies of the VDZ stood, and still stay, in the shadow of the other press associations, especially the BDZV. To be sure, it shares many common interests with the latter as revealed by their common distribution of an association organ *ZV + ZV*.

But that does not preclude the VDZ from making its own policy decisions in some cases. It did not go along with the broadcasting plans of the BDZV.[1] And it succeeded in having the distribution guidelines for European Recovery Plan credit[2] changed in their favour as these had previously favoured only daily newspapers.

The VDZ has been active especially in the area of the 'protection of youth' and censorship in developing a voluntary board of self-censorship. In order to protect children and youth from immoral publications, the federal government had a bill ready since 1949 which was intended to place extensive restrictions on such publications. The determination of immorality was to be incumbent upon state and federal examining boards to be made up of representatives from the ministries of the interior, the publishers, artists, and bookstore associations, the charity, youth, and education associations as well as from the religious communities. As a result of the protests of the VDZ, which were added to by other organizations, the 1953 'Schmutz und Schund' (Dirt and Trash) Law, or, more properly, the Harmful Publications Act, provided only for a federal examination agency. Later, the VDZ succeeded in having the term 'immoral' defined in more exact terms and thus reduced the danger of arbitrary decisions. However, the liberal judging practices of the examination agency proved the VDZ's early fears of it to be baseless.

In a parallel action, the VDZ concerned itself with the establishment of a voluntary board of self-censorship with a composition similar to that of the federal agency. However, this initiative had little effect. Finally, in 1957, the Self-Control of German Illustrated Magazines (SDI), later to become the Self-Control of Illustrated Magazines (SIZ) was founded as an institution extensively independent of the VDZ. It was composed of a segment of publishers and managing editors from the large illustrated magazines and a non-voting advisory council of representatives from the churches, youth, family and educational associations. It stopped its activities in 1964 because it had no sanctioning possibilities against a publisher other than expulsion from the SDI, and because disagreements between the publishers and the advisory council arose as well.

1. See Section 5.1.
2. cf. page 46.

A reorganization in 1966 gave a vote to the advisory council, but it was still a minority vote against that of the magazine representatives. Different publishers joined and resigned, and there were new organizational attempts such as the inclusion of different specialists. But the SIZ dissolved itself in 1971 as a consequence of the publishers' resignations.[1] The German Press Council has extensively exercised its functions since then.

In the beginning of the 1970s, the VDZ was put under increased pressure by both the journalists' organizations and the general public to transform itself into a legitimate business association with the bargaining authority to negotiate labour contracts. After offering some resistance, the VDZ gave in to these demands in 1972.

5.3 The German Journalists Union

The Deutsche Journalisten Union (DJU) (German Journalists Union) is what its name implies, that is, a journalists' union which is a daughter union of the Industrial Union for Print and Paper in the German Federation of Unions (DGB). The DJU has 3,750 members (1973).

The DJU was not always so strong as it is today, however. Despite a loose resource pooling with the German Journalists Association (DJV) and the German Employees Union (DAG) from 1953 to 1963,[2] it long remained in the shadow of the DJV, this due to the DJU's small membership. It was first recognized as a legitimate bargaining partner by the BDZV in 1966 and has since gained in both membership and stature.

In the past few years, the DJU has gone beyond the usual salary questions to deal as well with press concentration and to take a particular stance on the problem of 'inner' freedom of the press. It generally presents more far-reaching demands than the DJV. Thus, it has continually pleaded for a legislated regulation of the relationship between the publisher and the editorial staff, while the DJV favours negotiated solutions. Despite that, the DJU participated in negotiations over just such a contract which began in 1968. In June 1970, the journalists' and publishers' commissions finally agreed upon a contract that was intended to define the limits of publisher and editorial staff authority. But a national conference of the DJU rejected it in December 1970 because it saw the contract as containing too many of the publishers' recommendations and too few of the journalists'. At the same conference, the DJU developed a new contract that essentially demanded the following:
Protection for the beliefs of the editorial staff, that is, the right not to omit them, or to have to do, write or be responsible for anything contrary to those beliefs.

1. See Section 4.1.
2. This resource pool between the three unions was dissolved in 1963, after which an intense competition developed between the DJU and the DJV. Journalists' representation in the DAG has always been minor.

That the paper's basic position be determined by the publisher, established in writing and included in labour contracts.

That the guiding authority[1] rest with the editorial assembly, that is, the full editorial staff.

That the editorial staff should, after a hearing of the publisher, decide if a publication goes against the basic position of the newspaper.

That any changes in the paper's basic position, appearance, or editorial budget be possible only with approval of the editorial assembly.

That the editorial staff be regularly informed about the financial state of the paper.

That all changes in the paper's business form, property and stock relationships be brought before an editorial hearing.

That there be mandatory elections of editorial representation.

That the hiring or firing of the managing editor be done only with the approval of the editorial staff and that all other staff changes be approved by the elected editorial representation.

The BDZV rejected the union's proposal as being both illegal and unconstitutional as it would have taken away much of the publisher's constitutional rights to administer his property and even his own freedom of the press. The BDZV subsequently refused to bargain on the base of the DJU's proposal. The resulting deadlock lasted until August 1971, when all parties agreed to renew bargaining. New proposals at the base of the negotiations were drafted by all three journalists' organizations and went even further on the demands of the publishers than did those of the DJU.

Two primary sources of conflict between the publishers and journalists stood out in these negotiations: (a) the question of guiding authority, and (b) journalist participation in personnel administration.

All parties agreed that the basic guiding authority belongs to the publisher, that means the right to determine a publication's basic editorial position. They also agreed that the editor has the right to authority over the arrangement of editorial details, that is, detailed decision making, and that the publisher may issue no instructions as to editorial details. No agreement was reached on the guiding authority between those two positions. The journalists feared that their own decision-making position would be undermined if that were delegated to the publishers. In reverse, the publishers feared attempts 'to undermine their basic authority, because they were offered no possibilities for exercising direct influence upon the newspaper's position, even for the most important of reasons'.[2]

The journalists' demand for participation in personnel affairs revolves on the securing of their decision-making powers. Otherwise, a publisher could avoid an unfavourable reaction from journalist's sharing in decision making by either outright dismissal or transfer. On the other hand, the publishers saw in

---

1. That means the right to establish the paper's position on newly arising questions of a basic nature beyond those of ordinary, daily operations.
2. *Die Feder*, No. 6, 1972, p. 3.

the staff sharing of personnel authority a reduction of their own management rights and a weakening of the managing editor's position which would be subordinate to the confidence of the majority of the staff. Therefore, the publishers opposed the staff's right of veto in the hiring or firing of the managing editor, but are ready to concede certain hearing and information rights to the staff.

The negotiations are stagnating at this point in the discussions. Next to those points, there are discussions about the question of internal freedom of the press in conjunction with the 'frame' press law presently being drawn up by the German Federation in order to draft a few rough principles. However, some newspapers and magazines have recently agreed to so-called 'editorial statutes'. From case to case, they deal differently with the definition of authority and the regulation of staff participation.

5.4 The German Journalists Association

The Deutsche Journalisten-Verband e.V. (DJV) (German Journalists Association) is a professional association of practising journalists and editors and has approximately 9,000 members (1973).[1]

The DJV was giving precedence to media policy as early as the immediate post-war years. Even then, it had provoked discussion about introducing new business forms to the press. It recommended that alternatives such as foundations and co-operatives be developed to the traditional private press. Reasons for those recommendations were: (a) a belief that the private press had failed to fulfil its 'public duties in the immediate past'; and (b) the Allies' policies for licensing new publishers left open many questions about press property as most of the licensees had invested no personal capital in their publishing plants. These recommendations were punctured by the Allies' licensing regulations and found no sympathy with the post-war licensees who had quickly accustomed themselves to their new roles as publishers.

Highly visible press concentration led to renewed and serious discussions about the press' operating forms. The DJV again pleaded for the conversion of papers with a local monopoly into public foundations. The publishers contested this by arguing: (a) that only a private press is suitable for democratic society; and (b) that public foundations or similar forms lead to socialism, are not flexible enough and open the door to State and other influences. The journalists responded by emphasizing that the foundation form is especially suited for countering unprofessional, mostly business-motivated tampering with newspaper content.

As in the fifties, this discussion has led to no practical results, not one of the least reasons being the Federal Republic's very complicated foundation laws.

1. One cannot compare the memberships of the DJU and DJV because journalists from all the media are organized in the DJV, but only from the press in the DJU. The corresponding union for the electronic media is the RFFU. As regards the press journalists exclusively, both unions have approximately equal membership.

The DJV was more successful in its efforts to establish a voluntary board of self-control. After early discussion of a legislated board with executive authority, the DJV has tended more towards voluntary self-control since 1952–53. At that time, the DJV's Hamburg branch advanced the establishment of a control organ patterned after the British Press Council. After years of discussion revolving about the council's authority and composition,[1] representatives of the DJV and the BDZV founded the German Press Council in 1956. It is composed of proportional delegations from the newspaper and magazine publishers' and journalists' associations (DJV and DJU) and its purpose is:
To protect the freedom of the press, and ensure journalists' unhindered access to news sources.
To determine and dispose of abuses in the press.
To observe the structural developments in the German press, and to protect against business and monopoly developments that endanger a free press.
To formally represent the German newspaper press before the government, the parliament, the general public, and in any bills directly affecting the existence and duties of the press.
As an organ of self-control, the Press Council is primarily a moral authority because it lacks any manner of executive authority or sanctioning powers. Contrary to the original conceptions of the publishers, the Press Council has developed a certain independence from its parent organizations. Despite its missing authority, the council has gained both standing and influence especially by the compilation of press ethics and by co-operating with the German *Länder* in drafting state press laws.

Like the DJU, the DJV has also developed detailed conceptions about the shape of the publisher–editor relationship. In 1953 it presented the draft of a press law which would have ensured that precedence of news reporting over a newspaper's basic position be included in all wage contracts, and that any editorial staff member suddenly fired be entitled to draw a continuing salary after release that would equal up to a year's pay. In addition, it would have guaranteed the staff a voice in any management decisions that directly affected it. As the DJV draft is more flexible than that of the DJU, it is still, even today, suitable as the basis of an agreement between the publishers and journalists. But both this draft and the following recommendations of the DJV for negotiated settlements have never been realized.

The DJV long stood much closer to such negotiated settlements than did the DJU with its emphasis on the legislated regulation of the publisher–journalist relationship. However, shifts in the DJV policy have recently become noticeable. Thus, the DJV's proposals presented in March 1970 included provisions for a press law that would regulate the delegation of authority between the publisher and the editorial staff. In face of the fact that the law-

---

1. The newspaper publishers at first resisted the inclusion of magazine publishers on the German Press Council.

givers were expecting a negotiated settlement about those relations, the DJV took part in the latest negotiations about just such a contract with the BDZV.[1]

5.5 The PEN Centre of the Federal Republic of Germany

The German PEN Centre of the Federal Republic was founded in 1951 and changed its name in 1972 to the PEN Centre of the Federal Republic of Germany (PEN-Zentrum Bundesrepublik Deutschland). The organization now has approximately 350 members. Heinrich Böll, who was the German organization's leader in 1970 and 1971, has been president of the International PEN since 1971.

Conditions for acceptance into the Federal Republic's PEN are: (a) a belief in the PEN charter's plea for peace, the understanding of humanity, and human rights, especially the freedom of belief; (b) previous publication of a major literary work in the German language.

The PEN in the Federal Republic of Germany has long been regarded as a type of academy of more or less important literary figures in their advanced years,[2] but has recently been going through certain changes. The centre now engages in direct political activity in addition to its traditional practice of supporting persecuted authors and books.

Thus the centre's 1971 assembly not only discussed such themes as 'literature and its market' but also 'literature of the working world and the class struggle' as well as 'the problems of pornography'. It decided to elect a judicially critical committee that would take critical issue with the political-legal judgements in the Federal Republic. And the question of press concentration was inserted into the programme of the next assembly.

After much discussion, the assembly of April 1972 in Dortmund criticized the 'guidelines to the question of constitutional enemies in the civil service' which were resolved by both the federation and the *Länder* on 28 February of the same year. The assembly resolved to renew yearly reports about persecuted authors everywhere, and to critically protest at the sentencing of the Soviet author Bukovski. It further protested against a change in the Bavarian Broadcasting Law which had intentional loopholes for increased party influence, against seizures that had been recently made in an editorial office in the Federal Republic, and against the sudden firing of a broadcasting employee because of a critical magazine article he wrote. On the other side, it passed resolutions favourable towards the republic's newly concluded eastern treaties, and formally greeted attempts by the Association of German Authors (VS) to reorganize along union lines.[3]

1. See Section 5.1.
2. Robert Neumann in the weekly newspaper *Die Zeit*, 21 May 1971.
3. See Section 5.7.

However, the 'politicalization' of the PEN brought its own problems. The General Secretary of the PEN felt bound to circulate a letter in which he warned against the formation of fractions in the PEN:

We should preserve the club character of the PEN and remain friends even if we are divided by political beliefs, disagreements about literary opinions, and, indeed, simple decisions of personal taste. The formation of fractions is all too often the beginning of schisms.[1]

5.6 The Radio-Television-Film Union

In 1950, the Group Radio was constituted as a branch of the Society of German Stage Members which belonged to the DGB as a member of the Art Union. The group already had its own administrative and financial sovereignity, but became an independent association in the Art Union in 1952. In 1960 it changed its name to the Radio and Television Union (RFU). It took over the German Union of Film Workers in 1968 and subsequently changed its title to the Radio-Television-Film Union in the German Federation of Unions (Rundfunk-Fernseh-Film-Union im DGB e.V. (RFFU)). With a current membership of about 15,000, 4,000 of whom are journalists, the union has organized about 70 per cent of those employed in the radio, television and film media.

The activities of the union extend beyond the usual salary policies into two other large areas: (a) ensuring the independence of German broadcasting from the influence of both State and private interest groups; (b) obtaining management participation by broadcasting employees.

Even in the fifties, it had objected to too much State influence in the interstate treaty establishing the South-west Broadcasting and in the broadcasting bill presented by the federal government in 1953. The RFFU fought against similar tendencies in the drafting of federal and state legislation to regulate broadcasting, and in attempts to revise a few *Land* broadcasting laws.

As it became clear that the federal government was attempting to establish a second German television network (ZDF) in collaboration with private production companies, the union protested, and demanded that a purely public broadcasting system be retained in the Federal Republic. This stance can be also found in the union's position on the federal government's broadcasting bill of 1959 which would have provided for the private programme production of a second German television network.

It consequently opposed Adenauer's German Television, Inc., an attempt to legally ban advertising carried by public broadcasting, attempts by the BDZV to take over production of ZDF and a 1967 change in Saarland's broadcasting law.[2]

1. A PEN membership letter dated 1 June 1972, p. 1–2.
2. See Section 5.1.

If the RFFU extensively agreed with the broadcasting institutes on all of the above, it had from early on appealed to them for closer co-operation inside the first German television network (ARD). According to the union, co-operation and extensive efficiency could solve such network problems as the financial accounting between the institutes, programme co-ordination, the development of an educational channel, the introduction of colour broadcasting, and even studies about the future of television. The union viewed careful efficiency measures as the only means of optimally defending the existing network structure from both State influences and attempts to change it.

The RFFU has also long concerned itself with the area of management participation. Even in the fifties, the union had advanced the 'participation and consultation by representatives of the shop council and the Radio Union on the broadcasting institutes' supervisory boards'.[1] Together with that, it attempted unsuccessfully to have the German Industrial Relation Law, with its extended participation rights, applied to broadcasting institutes where only the Personal Representative Law, with its reduced staff participation in management, is in effect. These efforts have been intensified since the mid-sixties. There has also been more union discussion about the hierarchic structure of the institutes with their 'one-man rule' of the superintendents and subsequent demands to distribute their power.

The RFFU is also sceptical about the editorial statutes that the journalists want for the individual institutes. The union sees such statutes as directly affecting the rights of the shop and especially the personnel councils.

To sum up, the RFFU today has the following goals:

(a) Extensive participation in personnel management all the way from hiring to firing;
(b) participation in the regulation of working conditions;
(c) participation in social welfare activities;
(d) participation in organizational decisions such as: work methods, shop material, production procedures, efficiency, position and organizational planning as well as network business distribution.

The RFFU attempts to be present with at least two representatives on each respective supervisory board. And, finally, in case the superintendent and personnel council reach no decisions on participation, the union demands the establishment of a settlement board composed of one or two representatives from each side and a jointly elected chairman.[2]

The union's film policies demand a revision of the Law for the Advancement of Film, which had as its criterion of support the amount of the distribution revenue.

The union negotiators are mainly concerned with securing a common wage system for broadcasting institutes and better social security for freelance co-workers. The union noted its first bargaining success in this area in the

1. *Hörfunk, Fernsehen, Film*, No. 6, 1968.
2. *Hörfunk, Fernsehen, Film*, No. 5, 1971, p. 17.

agreement for a combined pension plan for this group of journalists which embraces all institutes.

5.7 The Association of German Writers

The Verband deutscher Schrifsteller e.V. (VS) (Association of German Writers) was founded in 1969 and replaced the Federal Alliance of Writers Associations, which was a loose federation of thirteen writers' associations. With its founding, translators, authors and critics in the Federal Republic of Germany and West Berlin had a single association for the first time. Its 1973 membership stands at about 3,000.

The VS sees its functions as: (a) social (for example, securing old-age pensions and supporting needy and young authors); (b) legal/copyright (for example, payment for reprints in schoolbooks and lending by libraries); (c) monetary (for example, issuing contract guidelines, lobbying for tax relief); (d) socio-political (for example, socially critical or political engagement). The VS directed the main thrust of its activities to the problems of copyright law, old-age pensions, and to its own accession to a labour union.

It began supporting the levying of a so-called 'library *groschen*' (10 pfennig piece) on the lending of a book by public libraries. Half of the levied fees would go to a social fund; the other half being distributed to the authors according to a point system.

The levy proposal aroused much controversy. Its critics feared disproportionately large costs and too many problems with the statistical listing of all lendings. They also raised the question as to who pays the *groschen* because cultural-political ethics make it improper to demand it of either the public libraries or the borrowers.

A further barrier to the *groschen* levy was the result of a query into the financial state of writers. It revealed that the authors are generally no worse off than the average populace. The VS countered by stating that 33 per cent of the freelance authors earn less than DM.1,000 in monthly commissions and fees, and that 27 per cent can expect neither pensions nor social security.

On 14 June 1972 the Bundestag passed the VS's desired amendments to the copyright law. They provide for the 'library *groschen*' and oblige schoolbook publishers to honour excerpts out of literary works.

The VS has not yet achieved its goal for the reclassification of the authors' legal status. Authors are still classed as independent businessmen and are accordingly taxed as such. The VS demands their legal recognition as 'persons similar to employees' through a change in the labour laws, because the majority of writers are really not 'independent' but receive their commissions from a single employer, mostly broadcasting institutes.

The question of associating with a union led to serious conflicts in the VS. Its first assembly in November 1970 already charged the chairman with developing a suitable organization model.

In the following discussion, proponents of the union alliance emphasized that the strong position needed to achieve their social and political goals could only be attained by solidarity with all media employees, including printers, typesetters, etc., who are mainly organized in the Industrial Union of Print and Paper.[1] Therefore, reduction of the VS's independence by union accession would be acceptable. The opponents of union accession counter-attacked by arguing that independence would be lost, and that there was a danger of the authors' being marshalled about by the members of the other unions, because, as union members, expressions critical of unions would only be conditionally possible.

An organization plan was developed in intensive talks between the VS and the Industrial Union of Print and Paper. It provided for a certain independence of the VS in the latter. There was also concurrent discussion about accession to the Art Union which certainly offered more independence but less effectiveness. In the beginning of 1973, the second Writers' Congress voted to accede to the Industrial Union of Print and Paper. The success of that move remains to be seen, because contrary to the original expectations of the VS, corporative accession is not possible and each VS member may only join the union on an individual basis.

Because of the differences over the union question, a Bavarian fraction of accession opponents was formed which finally separated from the VS.

Altogether, the union accession of the Association of German Writers is still the first step towards developing an Industrial Union of Media for all media employees.

1. The Industrial Union of Print and Paper (I.G. Druck und Papier) has about 150,000 members (1973). The DJU is also a member organization.

6 The state of journalists' training and education

As in most other West-European countries, one can distinguish three different paths leading to the journalistic profession in the Federal Republic of Germany:

On-the-job professional training: This is a completely practice-orientated apprentice training conducted by newspapers, magazines, broadcasting stations, news agencies, etc. It is supplemented by voluntary participation in so-called voluntary courses in theory which are organized and conducted by the journalists' and publishers' associations and by the broadcasting institutes.

Professional training: The German Journalists' School in Munich was founded in 1959 and remains the only non-commercial institute of its type in the Federal Republic of Germany. It trains 'gifted young talent for the journalist's profession in all of the public media'. It enrols thirty students per year and trains them in a fifteen-month period, eight months of which are devoted to theoretical education and six months of which are given over to practical training. The school's curriculum is concerned with 'expanding the training in contrast to the apprentice programme and thus compensating for the fluctuation of journalists between the media'.

Further, there are two recently founded institutes for the area of audio-visual media: Deutsche Film- und Fernsehakademie in Berlin (German Film and Television Academy in Berlin) founded in 1965; and Hochschule für Fernsehen und Film in München (mit der Abteilung I: Kommunikationswissenschaft und Studium generale) (College for Television and Film in Munich Section I: Communications science and general studies) founded in 1966. Both of these film and television academies serve mainly to prepare students for careers in film and television production.

Basic professional education in the framework of university courses: Journalism and communication research are presently being taught at the following universities in the Federal Republic of Germany including West Berlin: Institut für Publizistik der Freien Universität Berlin (Institute for Journalism at the Free University of Berlin); Sektion für Publizistik und Kommunikation an der Ruhr-Universität Bochum (Institute for Journalism and Communication at the Ruhr University of Bochum); Institut für Publizistik der Universität Göttingen (Institute for Journalism of the University of Goettingen); Institut für Publizistik der Universität Mainz (Institute for Journalism of the

University of Mainz; Institut für Zeitungswissenschaft der Universität München (Institute for Communications Science of the University of Munich); Institut für Publizistik der Universität Münster (Institute for Journalism of the University of Muenster); Institut für Politik und Kommunikationswissenschaft der Universität Erlangen-Nürnberg (Institute for Politics and Communications Science of the University of Erlangen-Nürnberg).

The courses offered at the above universities serve as a preparatory, professional education, not as practical professional training. Over 3,000 students are presently estimated to be majoring or minoring in journalism or communications science, and that number is growing.

The situation of journalists' training and education in the Federal Republic of Germany points to the following basic questions:

Divisions between the different methods of journalists' training and education, i.e. apprenticeship, journalists' school and the universities.

A complete lack of professionally orientated studies which could compare with corresponding institutions in other countries.

A lack of scientific orientation in the professional training.

A discrepancy between the number of students (and the number of practical professional desires that can be inferred from it) and the course offerings, physical equipment, and the personnel capacities of the few university institutes for journalism and communications science.

The discussion about the education and training of journalists has been carried on for years, and the most important arguments are summed up in the following theses:

The problem of training for the journalistic profession is a problem for the whole of society.

Entrance to the different journalistic professions is not bound to any training criteria and has thus impaired the journalists' mobility and independence. Educational preparation for the profession in the schools and universities is both spotty and insufficient. That, and the often one-sided professional education of many practising journalists, endangers the democratic function of the mass media.

The many-sided duties of today's journalists make it essential that professional training and post-graduate, advanced education be substantially improved in a democratic society.

Due to practical professional and socio-political reasons, a balanced and scientific education is indispensable to the communications professions.

A wide offering of educational chances and an extensive academic upgrading of the journalists' education should not restrict or regiment entrance into the profession.

A contract which was signed only in 1969 between the journalists' organizations and the daily newspapers, and which provides for a regulated voluntary apprenticeship, leaves, with its minimum regulations, no expectation for any basic improvement in journalist apprenticeships.

The present education capacities in the Federal Republic of Germany are insufficient to fulfil the rising demand for qualified journalists.

Next to basic journalistic education, an advanced education accompanying professional practice should be strongly considered in prospective educational policies.

Resulting from these tendencies, there is the demand that journalistic training and continuing training be fully integrated and correspondingly expanded in the public institutions for journalism and communications science. That means that apprentice programmes and journalists' schools should be integrated into the scientific, professional education programmes of the universities.

The restructuring of the institutions of journalist training and post-graduate education within the universities must take into account:

Growing demands put on most journalistic professions as regarding: (a) general education; (b) professional ethics; (c) professional training in specialized areas; (d) knowledge of the media; (e) communications theory.

Rapid and technically conditioned changes in professional realities.

Growing personnel needs in the continually differentiated institutions of social communication.

Newly developing professional fields (educational and leisure areas).

An increased basing of education for all professions in modern industrial society upon scientific concepts.

The small capacity of existing facilities for the education of journalists.

Reforming journalists' education and training in the framework of state measures can be accomplished by expanding and improving existing educational possibilities.

Facilities for advanced training must be newly planned to contain: (a) possibilities for advanced training in the universities; (b) facilities for contact studies of journalism and communications science in co-operation with other special academic areas; and (c) possibilities for correspondence courses at the university level.

In 1970, the German Press Council took the initiative to call a Commission for Questions of Journalistic Education and Advanced Education into existence. It presented a Memorandum for Journalists' Education in January 1971. In the two years since it was issued, it has catalysed the following moves:

The media policy papers of the political parties contain, as a central goal, the improvement of journalists' education.

In discussions and resolutions, the professional associations and broadcasting institutes have recognized the need for a practice-orientated and scientific education on the university level for their profession. This, after decades of rejecting the idea.[1]

Concrete reform plans were made by some of the *Länder* in the Federal Republic of Germany:

---

1. German Journalists Union (DJU): conferences in Mainz and Springen, October and November 1973; German Journalists Association (DJV): Association Assembly in 1973; the first German television network (ARD) created a commission for training new journalists in September 1973.

Berlin: the Berlin model creates a practice-orientated course of study and establishes the study of journalism as a *Zweitstudium* (a second, post graduate course of study) after completing another course of study in specialized areas.

Bavaria: the Munich model establishes co-operation between the German Journalists' School and the Institut für Zeitungswissenschaft (Institute for Communications Science) of the University of Munich; it is a model attempt for achieving practice-orientated study in the area of communication science.

Mainz: A model for journalists' education has been presented by the Cultural Ministry of Rheinland-Pfalz. The training should combine university studies with practical training in the media and other organizations.

Nordrhein-Westfalen: recommendations for educational reforms in the area of journalists' education were issued by the Council for Education Reform of the Ministry for Science and Research of the *Land* Nordrhein-Westfalen (1972). In addition to that, there is co-operation between the Cologne School of Journalism and the University of Cologne.

Corresponding but still fluid plans have been advanced in Hessen, Hamburg and Baden-Wuerttemberg. When prognoses are attempted it is to be expected that several model attempts will be instituted and executed, and major institutional reforms will be possible by 1980.

7 Media conceptions of the major political parties

7.1 The media concept of the SPD

As in the other political parties in the Federal Republic of Germany, the SPD's formulated programme had earlier given the mass media a subordinate role to play. Thus, in the Godesberger Programme,[1] only the following short paragraph on mass media is to be found:

Press, radio, television and film fulfil public requirements. They must be allowed to collect, process and distribute information, and develop and speak opinions that they are responsible for, in freedom and independence without hindrance everywhere. Television and radio must retain their public character. They must be freely and democratically directed and protected against pressure of interest groups.

However, in its 1971 convention in Bonn, the SPD became the first party in Germany to pass a resolution on a detailed media concept which is since binding for the SPD.[2] At the beginning of the convention, the chairman of the Mass Media Commission, Heinz Ruhnau, sketched the following points of departure for the SPD's media policy:

The reasons for press concentration and its effects in the local and regional areas, as well as the danger of abusing journalistic power.

'Control of journalistic power may never interfere with the right of free expression'.[3] The most effective control is that of journalistic opposing power, as is approximately demonstrated by the public broadcasting institutes. These leading ideas should be further developed and applied to the local and regional areas.

The democratic State may only carry out communication policy interference in order to protect the freedom of the individual, and not to restrict communications freedom for the benefit of the State.

---

1. The SPD guiding programme which was established in 1959 and which is still valid today.
2. The resolution on the state and the development of the mass media in the Federal Republic of Germany. Passed by extraordinary convention of the SPD on 20 November 1971 in Bonn. Printed in a brochure distributed by the executive committee of the SPD, *The Mass Media*. An introductory paper given by Heinz Ruhnau and Resolutions of the Party Convention about Media Policy—Press, Radio, Television, Film and New Techniques', 1971. Hereafter cited as SPD Media Concept.
3. ibid., p. 7.

The recommended *Land* press committees should be free from the State and serve the extension of communications freedom, and not the constriction thereof. Measures such as merger control, the obligation to publicize business relationships, etc., also serve this purpose.

A separation of authority between the publishers and journalists and the latters' management participation are welcome goals, but they may not be misunderstood as special rights for the journalists. Their independence should also be extended by a uniform retirement plan and improved training and education.

'In no other area of politics is Max Weber's maxim about a sense of proportion so valid as it is for this of mass media policy. Here, it depends especially upon developing a concept that is realistic and tailored with this sense of proportion.[1]

Ruhnau finally recommends that the listeners, and viewers be more considered than before in media policy.

THE MOST IMPORTANT POINTS OF THE MEDIA CONCEPT

Journalistic independence and the press
The question of journalists' management participation became a central issue of the convention's media policy discussion, and it led to the following result:

The independence of journalistic labour must be institutionally ensured, therefore the authorities of the publishers, editors-in-chief and the journalistic staffs are to be separated from each other. The editorial staffs are to be given specific management participation rights, which may not contradict the principle of a unified employees' representation. If a negotiated regulation of this has not been achieved within a reasonable period of time, then a legislated regulation is to be striven for.[2]

The control of economic and journalistic power
'In order to counteract *abuses* of *information distribution* by the *monopoly* of a newspaper or a concern in any given *region*' the Media Concept of the SPD recommends supervision of such possible abuses by the creation of *Land press committees*.[3] Like the example of the broadcasting councils, they should be socially organized, independent of the state, and have the following rights and duties:

(a) to observe the development of determinable abuses and to publish their positions thereon;
(b) to judge complaints and to publish their own positions on them;
(c) to publish such positions in the plaintiff newspapers;
(d) to observe and make public any monopoly developments in the distribution sector.[4]

1. SPD Media Concept, p. 7.
2. ibid., p. 15.
3. ibid., p. 16; italics by the authors.
4. ibid., p. 16–17.

Complementing the strengthening of journalistic independence, measures to control and restrict economic concentration in the press should serve to preserve a diversity of opinion. To that end, the following press and monopoly law measures have been seen as suitable:

Obliging the press to make its journalistic stance and business relationships public.

Obligatory registration for mergers of newspaper and magazine undertakings (merger control). 'These mergers may be forbidden if they endanger or restrict the freedom of information and opinion, restrict competition, or promote the development of undertakings which control the market'.[1]

To secure the access to the distribution systems and the independence of the news agencies.

To maintain or revive the local/regional journalistic diversity.

To achieve a uniform retirement plan for the entire media area which would improve the mobility and thus the independence of journalists.

To improve journalistic education and training.

To improve the obligation of State organs to inform journalists.

Television and radio

There was little discussion about broadcasting at the convention because there was a consensus that the public and federalistic structure of broadcasting has proved itself. The convention further expressed opposition to all forms of putting broadcasting into private ownership and its commercialization. Such developments are to be hindered by corresponding changes in the law. *'This also applies to additional frequencies which may become available.* After the full providing of the people has been achieved with existing channels, the *additional frequencies* should be introduced with the *primary purpose of education.*[2]

According to the principle of 'journalistic balance' and 'journalistic opposing power' broadcasting in the regional and local areas has been accorded an essential task: 'Journalistic balance in this area can be maintained or restored by an extension of broadcasting time, a spreading of regionally and locally aimed programmes or by introducing new local and regional channels.[3]

In order not to endanger the economic position of newspapers, such channels should not be given over to newly created, independent broadcasting institutes, but to the existing broadcasting institutes which would finance such channels exclusively through fees.

The SPD Media Concept recommends the following for the internal structure of broadcasting:

Restricting the directive rights of the superintendents in favour of strengthened co-responsibility of the journalists; dismantling the hierarchic structure in favour of the colleague principle.

1. SPD Media Concept, p. 17.
2. ibid., p. 18; italics by the authors.
3. ibid., p. 18.

Securing management participation through editorial statutes and the inclusion of employee representatives of the broadcasting institutes on their executive councils.

That all sittings of the broadcasting councils be held in public.

That all broadcasting institutes make a yearly statement of account that at least corresponds to corporate law provisions.

New electronic media

With the introduction of new audio-visual media, the SPD favours a competition of public and private cassette production and public cable systems which, for example, would serve the purpose of transmitting newspaper facsimiles and long-distance data processing.

In the area of education, the application of new information and educational techniques (for example, multi-media courses of study) should be supported and taken over by public organizations.

Film

The existing system of film support should be altered to favour films which are more socially critical and of higher artistic value. Therefore, the support may no longer be made dependent upon commercial income.

Movements such as 'communal cinema' are to be supported and institutes for film censorship (the FSK and the censorship of the Federal Bureau for Commercial Business) are to be abolished.

A Federal Commission for Communications

A Bundeskommission für das Kommunikationswesen (Federal Commission for Communications) 'is to be established either through an interstate treaty orthrough an extension of Community Duties according to Article 91–A of the Constitution, and is for the *advising* of State organs in decisions in the area of communications and for *publicly* explaining communication policy relationships. It is to insure that the free flow of information essential to the judgement of all citizens is not hindered by the abuse of journalistic and economic power.'[1]

This commission has been conceived with reference to the example of the American Federal Communications Commission (FCC), and is to be called up by the Federal President upon recommendation by the Federal Parliament (Bundestag) and Federal Council (Bundesrat).

The following functions have been conceived by the SPD as especially belonging to its assignments: publishing a yearly report about the state and development of the mass media; keeping statistics on the mass media; supporting communications research; giving consultation in the economic support of the press; establishing the amount of the broadcasting fees; participating in merger control; surveillance of super-regional newspaper monopolies against possible abuses.

1. SPD Media Concept, p. 22; italics by the authors.

The obligation of the resolutions
The media concept of the SPD is binding for its members and obliges them to contribute towards realization. The federal government is urged to 'immediately' introduce corresponding legislation in the framework of its press law possibilities. SPD fractions and governments in both the federation and the *Länder* have been similarly urged to take legislative action in their areas.

7.2 The media concept of the CDU/CSU

As of October 1973 neither the CDU/CSU (Christian Democratic Union/ Christian Socialist Union) nor the FDP (Free Democractic Party) had any media concepts binding upon their members. However, both published 'media papers' in 1973 which were to be voted upon in their party conventions in November 1973 (FDP) and in the spring of 1974 (CDU/CSU).[1] They shall only be shortly described here because of their still tentative character.

The most pessimistic situation analysis is the basis of the SPD Media Concept. Its catalogue of State and social control measures is therefore the most extensive in comparison to those of the other parties.

An essentially more positive description of the situation prevails in the CDU/CSU media paper. Its programme recommendations therefore remain in the background, and mostly contain appeals for professional ethic guidelines, for duty and individual responsibility as well as the hope for an extensive self-regulation and self-control of the media systems.

About one-third of the paper's solution recommendations are rejections of the recommendations made by other groups or parties. Two-thirds of it are from their own positively formulated goals. Recommendations for protecting the positively valued *status quo* and warnings against feared changes through State interference take a comparatively large space in the paper.

The media paper from the CDU/CSU primarily contains the following recommendations:
The creation of editorial staff committees in the press. These are intended to advance 'partner-like' co-operation between the publisher and the editorial staff through the hearing rights of the journalists. Similar recommendations have been made for broadcasting.
Improving the training and education of journalists as well as their old-age security.
State economic support to counter press concentration.
Increasing the authority of the German Press Council.

---

1. CDU/CSU, 'The Media Paper of the CDU/CSU. Presented by the Media Commission of the CDU/CSU. Draft of the Media Commission', in *CDU diskutiert*. [June 1973.] FDP, *Guidelines for a Liberal Media Policy. A Presentation of the FDP Media Commission to the FDP Federal Executive Committee with Minority Recommendations. 3rd Version: The Results of the Final Committee Sittings on 21 June and 2 July 1973*. (Draft.)

Increased efficiency in and co-operation between the broadcasting institutes, as well as examining the question if other forms of broadcasting organization may develop besides the public form.

The private ownership organization of the new audio-visual media.

Maintenance of the existing film support and extending it by purposeful support measures for raising the quality of film.

7.3 The media concept of the FDP

In the FDP media paper, the situation analysis has only a secondary place. In its place are numerous and often very detailed recommendations for specific regulations. Almost half of them concern themselves with the problem of 'internal media freedom' and recommend extensive management participation rights for the news staffs.

The most important points in the FDP's programme are:

Strict maintenance of the division between public broadcasting and the private press.

Press law regulation of 'internal freedom of the press', especially:

(a) Obligatory editorial statutes.

(b) Elected editorial staff representation.

(c) A strict separation of the publishers', editors-in-chief's, and editorial staffs' authorities, where the authority to establish the basic principles lies with the publishers, the authority to establish guidelines for newly arising problems lies with the editors-in-chief, and detailed decision making lies with the editorial staff.[1]

(d) That the editorial staff have management participation rights in basic journalistic, economic and personnel changes.

Editorial statutes and elected editorial staff representation in broadcasting are analogous to the FDP's recommendations for the press, while taking into account the specific principles of the public broadcasting institutes.[2]

(a) A collegiate type of direction for broadcasting instead of the present, single direction by the superintendents.

(b) The composition of the supervisory boards should, in the future, comprise: one-third political party representatives; one-third socially relevant groups; one-third other personalities, to include experts and members of the audience.

Press concentration. If journalistic competition is endangered, the following measures are to be taken:

(a) Preventative merger control.

---

1. For these and further details about editorial statutes, compare with Sections 5.1–5.4 and 8.2.
2. cf. Section 8.1.

(b) Executive authority and the authority to impose sanctions for the German Press Council.

Further, the FDP recommends a voluntary, co-operative or public distribution.

The media paper of the FDP does not contain all of the problems treated in those of the SPD and the CDU/CSU, but it is the most detailed in its regulation of internal media freedom and press concentration.[1]

---

1. The media paper outlined here was passed without essential changes by the FDP convention on 13 November 1973 in Wiesbaden, and therefore became the binding media concept of this party.

8 Broadcasting organizations and their inner freedom

8.1 The public broadcasting system

The broadcasting order in the Federal Republic of Germany is characterized by federal departmentalization, public holding and the principle of social control.

The federal structure of the Federal Republic is mirrored in the federally departmentalized broadcasting system. Nine public broadcasting systems were established either by *Land* law or interstate treaty,[1] and, in 1950, these joined together to form the Working Association of Public Broadcasting Institutes in the Federal Republic of Germany (ARD). In their regional areas, these institutes broadcast radio programmes (1973, three channels each), a third, primarily educational TV channel, regional programming, and, after eight o'clock, national programming on the first television channel. Against the regional structure of the ARD network, there is a central network, the second German television (ZDF), which was founded by an interstate treaty between the *Länder*.[2] The 'territorial division of power' in this federalistic structure is seen as an essential guarantee for the independence of broadcasting.[3]

Public Institutes (Gemeinnützige Anstalten des öffentlichen Rechts) are the holders of the broadcasting systems. The type of public institute has been considerably modified to this end. The holders of the institutes, the *Länder* and the federation respectively, have less power of interference than in other public institutes; they have no directive rights, no authority for a continuous control of the institutes' organs, and no obligations for their financial support.[4] The broadcasting institutes have the right to self-control and are not subjected to State supervision of programming but only to legal supervision.[5] Their economic autonomy should be guaranteed by financing through levied fees and is

---

1. South-west Broadcasting (SWF) and North German Broadcasting (NDR) were established by interstate treaty.
2. Further, German Radio (Deutschlandfunk) and German Wave (Deutsche Welle) were founded as institutes under the authority of the federal government in 1960. These have a special status and somewhat different principles apply to their organization.
3. Peter Glotz, 'Das foederative Prinzip und die Rationalisierung im Rundfunkwessen', *Rundfunk und Fernsehen*, No. 4, 1967, p. 380–1.
4. Guenter Herrmann, 'Die Rundfunkanstalt. Eine Studie zum heutigen Rechtzustand', *Archiv des Öffentlichen Rechts*, Vol. 90, 1965, p. 299–300.
5. ibid., p. 308 et seq.

complemented by the budgetary self-control of the broadcasting institutes.[1] In addition, revenues from broadcast advertising have become an essential part of the institutes' financing.[2]

A distinctive and decisive feature of the broadcasting order is its legally anchored social control which is intended to be realized through pluralistically composed supervisory boards. It is intended that representatives of all meaningful political, social and ideological (religious) groups should be included on the supervisory boards. The Federal Constitutional Court has confirmed that these groups have, through their participation on the boards, 'the power to control the authoritative and co-decisive powers responsible for programming and therefore to correct them accordingly, so that enough will be done to fulfil the legal guidelines for a proportional inclusion of all those interested in broadcasting'.[3] This broadcasting structure is intended to ensure that all social groups are represented in, and have access to, broadcasting. This is not intended to achieve a 'neutrality' of broadcasting which is equivalent to a complete lack of any position, but a balanced consideration of the different opinion positions in society.[4] The supervisory boards are accordingly granted extensive participation rights.

The highest organ of the broadcasting institute is the broadcasting council, or the respective television council in the second German television. It is conceived as being the representative of the public interest in the broadcasting area. It usually has the right of electing the institute's superintendent[5] and of advising him in questions of programming while supervising compliance to programming guidelines. It determines the institute's budget, and has, in most cases, statutory authority.[6] The functions of the broadcasting councils are altogether 'those which are comparable to those of the legislative in the area of the State organization'.[7]

1. Herrmann, op cit., p. 302 et seq.
2. cf. information given in the Appendix.
3. Judgement of the Federal Constitutional Court, 2 February 1961. 'Fernseh-Urteil' [Television Judgement], *Rundfunk und Fernsehen*, No. 2, 1961, p. 181. (2BvG 1/60 and 2BvG 2/60.)
4. This is similarly expressed by Guenter Herrmann, '. . . Neutrality in the sense of broadcasting laws does not mean sterility, but a balance of the total programming through the integration of the most manifold expression of opinions possible.' 'Rechtsfragen der Rundfunkorganisation', *Rundfunk und Fernsehen*, No. 3, 1971, p. 279.
5. The superintendents of the NDR and WDR are elected by their executive councils. The superintendent of the SWF is elected by both the broadcasting and executive councils.
6. The statutes of the SFB and SDR are enacted by their respective *Land* legislatures; the statute authority at the BR and SWF lies with both the broadcasting and executive councils.
7. cf. Klaus Stern and Herbert Bethge, *Öffentlichrechtlicher und privatrechtlicher Rundfunk. Rechtsgutachterliche Untersuchung der Verfassungsmaessigkeit des Zweiten Gesetses zur Änderung und Ergaenzung des Gesetzes Nr. 806 über die Veranstaltung von Rundfunksendungen im Saarland vom 7. Juni 1967* [Public and Private Broadcasting. A Judicial Examination as to the Constitutionality of the Second Law for Revising and Amending Law No. 806 About the Organization of Broadcasting Programmes in Saarland from 7 June 1967], p. 66, Frankfurt and Berlin, 1971.

The superintendent heads the 'executive' branch of an institute, representing it externally, and running its business according to the decisions of the broadcasting and executive councils.

The executive council has the primary duties of supporting and supervising the superintendent's executive activities. The executive council has further authority, especially at the NDR and WDR, where it is the executive council, and not the broadcasting council, which elects the superintendent and controls adherence to the programme guidelines. These two institutes have a fourth organ in the programming co-council with authority restricted to advising the superintendent in programme development.

The selection and composition of the supervisory boards are regulated in varying fashion. The broadcasting council elects all or a majority of the members of the executive council. There are two different principles for the composition of a broadcasting council: the estate and the parliamentary model. According to the estate model, which is to be found in a majority of broadcasting institutes, different social groups, institutions and organizations send their delegates to sit with political party delegates in the broadcasting council. According to the parliamentary model which is applied at the NDR and WDR, members of the broadcasting council are elected by the respective *Land* legislative bodies without any specific legal regard for a pluralistic composition. Both of these institutes have an additional programming co-council which is composed along estate lines and whose members are usually summoned upon the recommendation of the delegating organizations.[1]

The basic principle of social control over broadcasting by the creation of special supervisory boards is extensively accepted today, at least for the existing institutes. However, it appears to many that there are problems in the concrete application of this principle.[2] 'The practice makes it quite clear that the boards established on the estate-pluralistic basis, even if they occasionally operate with difficulty, leave broadcasting employees more independence, while the legislative, politically elected boards are increasingly becoming transmission belts for political influence in the institutes.'[3] But, even the estate-pluralistic board construction does not exclude political superimpositions on the institutes.[4] The quality of board members is less decisive than the principle of social control; it is essential to 'interest enough responsibly thinking and acting personalities to work on the broadcasting boards'.[5] It appears to many critics that an essential weakness in the estate system is the fixed regulation of

1. cf. Klaus Peter Jank, *Die Rundfunkanstalten der Länder und des Bundes. Eine systematische Darstellung ihrer organisatorischen Grundlagen* [The Broadcasting Institutes of the Länder and the Federation. A Systematic Description of their Organizational Bases], p. 37–8, Berlin, 1967.
2. cf. Wolfgang R. Langenbucher and Walter A. Mahle, "Umkehrproporz' und kommunikative Relevanz', *Publizistik*, No. 4, 1973, p. 322–30.
3. Manfred Jenke, 'Alle Macht den (Rundfunk)-Raeten? Überlegungen zur Arbeit der Aufsichtsgremien der Anstalten', *epd/Kirche und Fernsehen*, No. 8, 27 February 1971.
4. ibid.; cf. also Gisela Hundertmark and Klaus Winckler, 'Rundfunkkontrolle und Parteieneinfluss', *Publizistik*, No. 4, 1973, p. 331–43.
5. Jenke, op. cit.

the catalogue of social groups to be represented on the broadcasting boards. 'This fixing in law and statutes cements the spectrum of socially relevant powers and does not account for the reality that the group's social position changes over the years, that, above all, new important groupings appear, and therewith their significance changes for the control function over broadcasting'.[1] Next to the moderately numbered and restricted membership of legislative bodies, governments and political parties in it, an ideal state supervisory board should provide for direct delegation rights of the social groups, not subjected to inadmissable attempts at influence. In order to remove the immobility in the composition of the represented groups, the broadcasting council should itself decide which groups should belong to it.[2] Another proposal suggests that fossilization of the estate boards should be prevented by admitting even small parties to the boards and obtaining a portion of the members by co-option of the broadcasting councils.[3]

One of the positions basically opposed to the current proportional concept for the composition of the broadcasting councils proceeds from the point that 'broadcasting should be a part of an open *communications system* that is as independent of the social *power structure* as possible, [and that] the independence of the communications system . . . is an essential condition for the mobility of the political system and subsequent democratic change'.[4] The following conclusion is drawn from that:

The choice of socially relevant groups should not be, at least not exclusively, made according to their social importance (power, size, etc.) but according to the criterion as to how far the respective groups' chances of access to public communication are endangered. This communications sociological selections criterion may be generally formulated: *the access chances of group to the broadcasting council should be inversely proportional to its access chances to public communication.*[5]

The criticisms and resultant recommendations for reform reviewed above are not all representative but should illustrate that the present form of the public broadcasting organization is not without its problems and is even considered ripe for reform by many of its defenders. However, their criticisms do not question the basic principles of broadcasting order: the federalistic structure, the organizational form of the public institute, and the institutionalized social control. This form of broadcasting organization is intended to guarantee the institutional autonomy of broadcasting, and the freedom of broadcasting from the State and single groups. Its advantages are comprehensively seen in the

1. Michael Schmid-Ospach, 'Gesellschaftliche Kräfte in der Rundfunkaufsicht: per Zufall? Überlegungen zur Zusammensetzung von Rundfunkraeten', *epd/Kirche und Rundfunk*, No. 27, 26 July 1972.
2. ibid.
3. Peter Glotz and Wolfgang Langenbucher, *Funk und Fernsehen in der Demokratie.* A programme broadcast by the WDR on 14 July 1970.
4. Langenbucher and Mahle, op. cit., p. 324; italics by the authors.
5. ibid., p. 328; italics by Langenbucher and Mahle.

'uniting of the public character with a certain revenue, supervision, and resultant programme structure in which a relative programme diversity is at least guaranteed . . ..'[1]

The criticism of those groups which strive for privately owned broadcasting as an alternative or competition to public broadcasting is more extensive and thorough. This has been often cited in earlier chapters.[2]

8.2 Broadcasting organizations and their internal freedom

Since 1969, press and broadcasting journalists in the Federal Republic of Germany have been concerned about attaining management participation and a direct voice in decisions affecting their work.

These endeavors were induced in the late sixties by general liberalization trends sparked by the student protest movement and which affected a wide range of the 'cultural industries'. Journalists' management participation in the press is intended to mitigate the results of press concentration such as the example of selling a publication without giving previous notice to its editorial staff. Further, management participation by the editorial staff is intended to hinder or at least lessen the influence of a publisher's economic considerations on editorial content, thus fulfilling the citizens' right to comprehensive information.[3]

On the other hand, there are already institutionalized possibilities for society to influence the programming and personnel decisions of public broadcasting institutes through the supervisory boards composed of representatives from 'socially relevent groups'. However, there has been much recent criticism of the negative developments on the boards, such as the marshalling of the other social groups by the political parties, political influence on personnel decisions, and attempts to directly influence programming made by political party representatives.[4]

Broadcasting journalists in the Federal Republic of Germany view all of the above as restrictions upon their comprehensively informing the audience. And they see their efforts to obtain 'internal broadcasting freedom' as being

1. Thomas Ellwein, 'Die Öffentlich-rechtliche Konstruktion des Fernsehens', in Theo von Alst (ed.), *Millionenspiele-Fernsehbetrieb in Deutschland*, p. 19, Munich, 1972.
2. cf. chapters 2 and 3 and Section 5.1. The attempts at establishing private broadcasting have been copiously described by Harald von Gottberg, *Initiativen für ein privates Fernsehen in der BRD* [Initiatives for a Private Television in the Federal Republic of Germany], Master's thesis, Freie Universitaet Berlin, 1972; Helga Montag *Die, Geschichte der Bestrebungen zur Einrichtung eines privaten Rundfunks in der Bundesrepublik Deutschland (1947–1967)* [The History of the Attempts to Establish Private Broadcasting in the Federal Republic of Germany, 1949 to 1967], Master's thesis, Munich, 1973.
3. The attempts at journalist's management participation in the press and the development of editorial statutes in the Federal Republic of Germany are copiously described and analysed by Susanne Welzel, *Redaktionsstatuten, Zum Problem der inneren Pressefreiheit in der Bundesrepublik Deutschland*, Master's thesis, Munich, 1972.
4. cf. Section 8.1.

levelled against such developments. The concept of 'internal broadcasting freedom' developed parallel to that of 'internal freedom of the press' and is analogous to it. It refers to the 'arrangement of the internal spheres of broadcasting institutes'[1] and to ordering the relations between media co-workers, leading editors, the supervisory boards and, finally, the superintendents with their executive authority.

Editors engaged in management participation have suggested two ways to realize 'internal broadcasting freedom': first, that the management participation rights, or at least hearing rights of editors in editorial, personnel, organizational and financial matters, be fixed in an 'editorial' or 'editor' statute and that a full editorial staff assembly elect an 'editorial staff committee'. And, secondly, that changes be made in the corresponding *Land* laws and interstate treaties so that its employees are included on the supervisory boards: i.e. broadcasting, television and executive councils. These representatives are to inform the other board members about their problems, be informed and, eventually, take part in decisions.

The achievements of these efforts until 1972 in the nine *Land* broadcasting systems, the federal radio systems German Wave and German Radio as well as in the second German television network (ZDF) may be summarized as follows: since 1969, editorial staff assemblies have constituted themselves as the highest staff bodies of resolution in all of the broadcasting systems. The assemblies, in turn, elect editorial staff committees which are charged with drafting 'editorial statutes' and protecting the interests of the staff. The committees are further charged with negotiating the conditions of these statutes with the management, and with securing binding management recognition of them.

The reaction of the superintendents to the staff demands has varied widely from rejection and non-recognition of the editorial staff committee, as is the case at Saarland Broadcasting, to occasional concessions, and to full cooperation with the editorial staff, as is the case with the West German and North German broadcasting systems. According to a poll taken by the Lutheran Press Service (epd) in July 1971,[2] a majority of the superintendents regard the editorial statutes as unnecessary. They are not willing to have their legally based executive authority restricted by management participation rights of the editorial staffs. But they do see certain advantages that may result from the statutes such as possible improvements in inter-departmental communication and more administrative transparency. The superintendents' arguments against the statutes are primarily of a formal judicial nature in both content and form.

During the course of the negotiations between the editorial staffs and the superintendents, most of the editorial statute drafts were often changed. Demands for direct management participation were watered down to only

---

1. Wolfgang Hoffmann-Riem, *Redaktionsstatute im Rundfunk*, p. 28, Baden-Baden, 1972.
2. cf. *epd/Kirche und Rundfunk*, No. 32, 1 September 1971; and to *Hörfunk, Fernsehen, Film*, No. 5, 1971.

hearing and information rights of the staff so that statute recognition by the superintendents would not be excluded from the beginning.

The major points of a typical 'editorial statute' refer to the following rights of the editorial staff: the right to representation; the right to hearings and information; the right to publication; the right to veto; the right to editorial self-determination or participation in editorial policy making; the right to protection for the individual beliefs of the staff members.[1]

The different 'editorial statute' drafts usually contain a recognition of the editor's public duties as spelled out by the Federal Constitution, *Land* broadcasting laws, and interstate treaties. Most drafts contain provisions for participation in personnel decisions, and especially for choosing editors-in-chief, department managers, programme directors, etc. Early drafts also provided for a staff veto right in certain personnel decisions. But these provisions were stricken due to the danger of confrontation with the superintendents' authority, and because such demands are illusory in the light of the given legal conditions. The statute drafts of the ZDF and the WDR editorial staffs are the only ones which haven't withdrawn the demands for such veto rights. A further article in these particular statutes prohibits the forcing of any staff member to express opinions that are contrary to his own or to be held responsible for such. If any report is altered or dropped from the programme, the person responsible would have to obtain the author's consent to such action. The editorial staff committee is to be informed and given hearing about any decisions affecting the staff or the structure of programming.

According to its statute, the editorial staff committee of the ZDF also has the duty to work towards 'possible participation of the editorial staff committee in sittings of the television and executive councils and their respective committees'. This provides the second path towards management participation, namely the representation of the editorial staff, or, as it has been extended in almost all broadcasting institutes, of all employees on the supervisory boards. Representatives of the personnel council usually sit in on meetings of the television broadcasting and executive boards of most institutes.[2] But only 'the personnel representation laws' of Hessen and Bremen give further authority to the personnel council representatives. At the Hessen broadcasting sysem, two members of the personnel council have the right to advisory, but not voting, participation on the executive council, although at Radio Bremen the two personnel council representatives are voting members of the executive council.

In many institutes, the early movement for editorial statutes were opposed not only by the superintendents but by other co-workers as well. This was because many of the union-orientated personnel councils represented all personnel and only had authority over social affairs. Thus they saw a competitive danger in the new editorial staff representation. In the meanwhile, both

1. cf. Ansgar Skriver, *Schreiben und schreiben lassen. Innere Pressefreiheit—Redaktionsstatute*, p. 129, Karlsruhe, 1970.
2. cf. details in Hans Peter Ipsen, *Mitbestimmung im Rundfunk. Verfassungsfragen zur Mitbestimmung durch Belegschaftsvertreter in den Aufsichtsgremien der Rundfunkanstalten*, p. 21 et seq., Frankfurt am Main, 1972.

organs have worked out some co-operation in most institutes. In some, the editors have even shifted their entire activities to the personnel council with the editorial staff committee functioning as a subcommittee of the personnel council, no longer being considered as an equal body. This development grew out of the position of a few superintendents who rejected the idea of autonomous editorial staff committees and a management participation statute, but were ready to concede a certain information and hearing right to the staff and to recognize editorial staff representation in the form of a professional group to be considered as equal to the institutes other professional group representation. In the following institutes these mutual concessions on the part of both editorial staff and the superintendent led to establishing partial regulations which took effect either as service regulations issued by the superintendent, or as operation agreements between the superintendent and the personnel council:

Bavaria Broadcasting (BR): superintendent's service regulation No. 3/71, 'in consultation with the personnel council' reached on 1 October 1971.

South-west Broadcasting (SWF): guidelines for the co-operation with the personnel representatives, and general work rules, issued by the superintendent 'in agreement with the general personnel council' on 1 January 1972.

Free Berlin Broadcasting (SFB): service agreements over the construction, hearing, and information rights of the professional group representatives reached on 1 December 1971.

Second German television (ZDF): general guidelines for co-operation in the ZDF decreed as a service regulation by the superintendent and concurrently in effect as of 1 January 1973.

Similar efforts are being made at Saarland Broadcasting and RIAS (Radio in the American Sector) Berlin.

No statute drafts by the editorial staffs and passed by the staff assembly have yet been bindingly recognized through the formal signature of the superintendents. It presently appears that no broadcasting institute excepting the NDR, will soon decide the subject. The negotiations over an editorial statute at the NDR between the editorial staff and the superintendent were closed in October 1972, but the formal signing by the superintendent still has not occurred.[1] Other superintendents raised objections, fearing that 'signal effects' would be flashed to their own institutes by such a signing. While the superintendents continued to speak out in relative unison against the editorial statutes and staff participation on the supervisory boards, supported by the arguments of the institutes' lawyers, these statute efforts were supported by a majority of editors. However, it should be noted that the number of editors still actively engaged in the statute movement is very small. A poll of eighty editors taken in conjunction with a dissertation about power structures in West German Broadcasting (WDR) reveals that 54 per cent of those questioned do not see any immediate danger to internal freedom in broadcasting, but see the possi-

1. The statute has meanwhile been recognized by the NDR in 1973.

bilities of such dangers in the present organizational structure of WDR.[1] Twenty-five per cent believe that internal freedom in broadcasting is partially endangered, and approximately 9 per cent, almost all editors-in-chief, saw internal freedom of broadcasting guaranteed by the WDR's present structure. Approximately 79 per cent spoke out for regulating and securing the editorial assembly's recommended staff participation as a means of securing internal freedom. Approximately 19 per cent opposed the proposed staff participation. Critics of editorial statutes accuse the initiators of being less concerned with broadcasting freedom than with securing both privileges for the editorial staff and the right to broadcast their own personal opinions.[2] Further, the 'socialization of broadcasting' would be partially set back by any special participation rights of the editorial staff.[3] Other opposing arguments refer to the legally regulated hierarchic structure of the broadcasting institutes and to the final responsibility for programming that lies with the superintendents and contend that the rights of the editorial staff to management participation are illegal according to the presently valid *Land* laws and interstate treaties.

The editors defended their position against those arguments by retorting that democratic organizational and decision structures would benefit the freedom of broadcasting as well as the information of the citizens. Staff management participation that is institutionalized by statutes would aid in resisting one-sided political influence attempts by governments, parties or associations. The statutes also would protect broadcasting freedom by abolishing pressure on the individual editor's beliefs; by improving internal communications and the work climate of the institutes; by achieving a transparency in executive decisions which would favour rational and controllable decisions; by raising the balance and quality of programming, and by reducing production costs through more efficient methods.[4]

The opposition to representation of editors in the supervisory boards counter by bringing out especially the following arguments: a co-worker representation means self-control and contradicts the principle of public control; representation of editors on the boards is unneccesary as the staffs represent no socially relevent group, and their interests are already represented by other groups such as the churches or the unions. Moreover, there is a basic incompatibility of both staff and board membership according to valid broadcasting law, thus staff representation would violate the legally fixed separation of duties in the broadcasting systems.[5]

1. cf. Rüdiger Hoffmann, *Die Entwicklung von Organisations- und Machtstrukturen im WDR und das Selbstverstaendnis der Programmacher. 1945–1972*, Cologne, Diss, 1972. Quoted here from *epd/Kirche und Rundfunk*, No. 40, 8 November 1972.
2. So argues Superintendent Mai of the Saarland Broadcasting; cf. *Hörfunk, Fernsehen, Film*, No. 5, 1971.
3. ibid.
4. Similar arguments are to be found in Otto Wilfert (ed.), *Es geht nicht nur um Springer, Material und Meinungen zur inneren Pressefreiheit*, Mainz, 1968; Florian Hoener, 'Mitbestimmung-praxisnah und rechtlich moeglich', in Bernward Frank (ed.), *Fernseh-Kritik*, Vol. IV, p. 55, Mainz, 1972; Skriver, op. cit., passim.
5. cf. Ipsen, op. cit.

The following points favouring staff participation on the broadcasting boards are put forward: because some groups, such as political parties, were overrepresented on the boards, staff representation could have a balancing and extending effect. Because other professional organizations are represented on the boards, the broadcasting union also has a right to representation on them. Because the usual definition of 'socially relevent groups' is too narrow, it must be extended to include other groups not yet represented on the boards.[1] Because board members have received most of their information from the superintendents up until now, staff representatives could inform them more extensively. This information would strengthen, not weaken, the position of the supervisory boards.[2]

The editorial staff committees have been legitimized by the news staff, but have been granted no official recognition by the institutes superintendents. However, these committees are active at most institutes and see their most important duties as: negotiating the statutes and their implementation; improving inter-departmental communications; mediating in case of internal conflicts; securing a voice, especially participation, in personnel and programming decisions; making the news staff aware of the statutes' meaning; and establishing professional group representation of the editorial staff.[3] Next to their activities in the institutes, the editorial staff committees are drawing up positions in order to make the public aware of their problems. Thus, for example, the editorial staff committee of the ZDF has publicly demanded of the ZDF executive council that they be given a hearing over the hiring of both a new managing editor and a second commentator for the *ZDF Magazin* programme.[4] The editorial staff committee at the WDR recommended that the vacant superintendent's post be advertised.[5] The ZDF editorial staff committee also protested against the rosy picture of the internal structure of the network painted by the ZDF Superintendent Holzamer in the programme *Conversation with the Audience*, because the harmony it presented in no way represented the true situation at the ZDF.[6]

The state of broadcasting staff efforts at the end of 1972

In June 1972, representatives from the editorial staff committees convened at Ronneburg and passed the following resolution:

The attempts by political party groups to take an ever-growing control and influence over the programming of radio and television threatens to make it impossible for the news personnel to fulfil their legal duties. The members of the editorial staff com-

---

1. cf. Section 8.1.
2. cf. RFFU in *Hörfunk, Fernsehen, Film*, No. 5, 1971; Ipsen, op. cit., p. 13; Höner, op. cit.
3. According to a written poll taken by the AfK of all the editorial staff committees at the beginning of 1973.
4. cf. *Süddeutsche Zeitung*, 15 July 1971.
5. cf. *Süddeutsche Zeitung*, 27 November 1970.
6. cf. *Der Journalist*, Vol. 1, 1973.

mittees assembled for their third working conference at Ronneburg consider it their duty to inform the public about the threats to internal and external freedom of the press which lie in such tendencies. The precedents in the West German and Bavarian broadcasting institutes are only the latest examples of such threats. The elected representatives of the editorial staffs therefore demand of the superintendents that a legal anchoring of the editorial statutes be no longer delayed, and that by this they make a necessary contribution towards securing internal broadcasting freedom. The mass media cannot advance democracy if they themselves are not organized in a democratic fashion.[1]

It may generally be said that there are at present no possibilities either for a legal anchoring of the editorial statutes which formulate more than a mere information and hearing right or for amending broadcasting laws which bear on the editorial staffs' participation in management. The demands of the editorial staffs have been better received in the 'north' German systems such as the NDR and the WDR than in the 'south' German systems such as the SR, SWF, SDR, and the federal radio systems.[2]

In the autumn of 1972, the judicial commission of the ARD, which is comprised of the institutes' lawyers, clearly repeated its objections to both the co-workers' representation on the supervisory boards and the editorial statutes. ARD lawyers view the inclusion of co-workers on the institutes' control boards as damaging 'in an unconstitutional manner, the balance of social legitimacy and control by group representation';[3] as contradicting the democratic principle of social control, and as violating the principle of equality. The judicial commission expressed the following legal objections to the editorial statutes: editorial staff privileges fixed in the statutes could contradict the principle of equal treatment. Recognition of the statutes would mean imposing self-restrictions upon the superintendent which would be incompatible with his executive responsibilities. Those responsible for programming decisions also have the right to interfere in broadcasts. And freelance co-workers could not be allowed to be included under the statutes jurisdiction.[4]

1. Quoted from *epd/Kirche und Rundfunk*, No. 23, 28 June 1972.
2. cf. footnote 5, p. 69.
3. ARD Superintendent Bausch quoted in *epd/Kirche und Rundfunk*, No. 36, 4 October 1972; cf. also *Hörfunk, Fernsehen, Film*, No. 5, 1972.
4. cf. *epd/Kirche und Rundfunk*, op. cit.

Appendix

Sources

All tables for which no other source is given are taken from 'Daten zur Mediensituation in der Bundesrepublik', in a special of *Media Perspektiven*, August 1973, in which the following sources were quoted: *ARD-Jahrbücher*, Daten 1972 im Vorabdruck; *ZDF-Jahrbücher*; *Statistische Jahrbücher der BRD* and Angaben des Statistischen Bundesamtes; *Buch- und Buchhandel in Zahlen*; *Jahresberichte des ZAW, Werbung*; *Filmstatistische Taschenbücher* and Angaben der Statistischen Abteilung der Spio; Löhne, Preise, *Wirtschaftsrechnungen, Reihe 6: Preise und Preisindices der Lebenshaltung*; *IVW-Auflagenlisten*; Veröffentlichungen von Schmidt & Pohlmann, Gesellschaft für Werbestatistik, Hamburg; Helmut H. Diederich, *Konzentration in den Massenmedien*; *Systematischer Überblick zur Situation in der BRD*, Munich, 1973; Rudolf Eisenhardt, *Experimentelle Richtwerte deutscher Tageszeitungen*, Mannheim o.J., 1971; Rudolf Hofsähs, 'Zur Entwicklung der Gewinne bei Tageszeitungen', *Publizistik*, No. 1, 1969; M. Knoche and A. Zerdick, 'Zur wirtschaftlichen Situation der Tageszeitungen in der Bundesrepublik', *Media Perspektiven*, No. 4, 1973; *Media Perspektiven*; author's estimates.

Mass media in the Federal Republic of Germany

Section A: THE PRESS

TABLE 1. Trends in the number and circulation of
newspapers and periodicals

	Newspapers				Periodicals			
	Daily newspapers		Weekly newspapers		General interest		Technical	
Year (fourth quarter)	Number	Copies sold (millions)	Number	Copies sold (millions)	Number	Copies sold (millions)	Number	Copies sold (millions)
1962	540	16.4	14	2.8	246	41.0	400	14.3
1963	534	16.7	16	3.3	247	42.1	425	15.5
1964	537	19.8	14	1.0	242	43.3	444	15.9
1965	543	20.1	14	1.0	252	46.5	473	15.9
1966	532	21.0	15	1.1	249	49.2	531	16.7
1967	524	20.8	17	1.2	245	52.6	583	17.8
1968	516	20.7	17	1.2	235	56.3	598	18.2
1969	506	21.1	19	1.3	238	58.1	643	18.2
1970	491	20.5	18	1.3	237	60.3	666	19.3
1971	469	20.6	16	1.2	226	62.8	657	19.5
1972	459	20.6	17	1.6	229	62.6	668	18.3

Source: See notes on page 74.

TABLE 2. Structure of costs and revenue: daily newspapers in 1970 grouped according to circulation classes

	Circulation in thousands									
	5 or less (%)	5–10 (%)	10–15 (%)	15–25 (%)	25–50 (%)	50–75 (%)	75–100 (%)	100–150 (%)	150–200 (%)	250 or more (%)
Costs[1]										
Editing	14.2	14.3	14.6	15.7	16.9	16.4	15.4	15.0	14.5	13.6
Distribution	14.4	16.5	17.5	18.3	19.6	20.3	21.8	22.4	22.6	22.7
Advertising	12.3	12.4	12.5	12.8	13.2	13.3	13.5	13.7	14.0	14.7
Administration	6.1	6.4	6.5	6.6	6.4	6.5	6.7	6.7	6.7	6.7
Setting and printing	44.6	41.3	39.3	36.9	33.1	32.0	30.5	29.5	28.8	28.2
Paper	8.4	9.1	9.6	9.8	10.8	11.5	12.1	12.7	13.4	14.1
Revenue[2]										
Sales	31.4	31.5	31.1	31.3	30.0	29.9	29.9	29.5	28.8	28.0
Advertising	68.6	68.5	68.9	68.7	70.0	70.1	70.1	70.5	71.2	72.0
Profit[2]	1.2	2.5	3.0	4.4	5.9	7.4	8.7	10.0	11.7	14.0

1. As percentage of total cost.
2. As percentage of total revenue.

Section B: ADVERTISING

TABLE 3. Trends in advertising turnover of selected advertising media from 1952 to 1972 (in millions of DM.).

Year	Newspapers[1]	Periodicals/ Magazines	Television	Radio	Placards, billboards	Direct mail	Cinema	Personal contact	Total	Local ads in newspapers
				Advertising media						
1952	333.3	173.4	—	20.9	37.2	·	·	·	·	
1953	432.9	212.9	—	23.1	43.4	·	·	·	·	
1954	500.1	262.0	—	28.2	50.7	·	·	·	·	Up
1955	566.2	311.9	—	32.1	59.4	·	·	·	·	until 1967
1956	658.5	390.1	0.2	32.1	61.7	·		·	·	included
1957	898.4	487.7	3.7	39.1	68.7	·	78.0	·	·	in commu-
1958	981.4	556.4	12.0	42.4	67.9	·	97.4	·	·	nal; in
1959	1,074.0	644.7	56.8	52.3	74.6	·	105.5	·	·	thousands
1960	1,137.6	744.3	132.1	48.8	82.4		98.8	·	·	of millions
1961	1,356.2	986.7	221.8	52.6	96.2		88.8		·	of DM.
1962	1,403.2	1,097.4	261.8	55.9	104.6	79.7	80.4	1,100.0	4,203.0	
1963	1,510.6	1,244.7	366.0	84.4	109.4	81.7	77.8	1,200.0	4,654.0	
1964	1,899.0	1,393.0	374.2	83.6	152.0	89.6	65.2	1,350.0	5,206.6	
1965	1,932.6	1,507.0	470.9	91.5	182.0	95.8	64.2	1,800.0	6,143.8	
1966	2,105.9	1,696.0	537.7	103.5	194.9	106.1	85.6	2,271.8	7,086.7	
1967	2,190.7	1,717.9	557.8	134.5	215.8	111.7	84.1	2,417.9	7,410.2	
1968[1]	739.5	1,507.0	546.9	152.0	229.5	123.3	55.7	2,528.6	5,868.0	1.77
1969	933.0	1,643.9	641.0	196.7	257.6	141.2	60.0	2,857.3	6,720.7	2.05
1970	952.3	1,899.8	645.5	205.7	262.2	183.1	57.2	3,007.6	7,288.4	2.17
1971	1,063.0	2,035.0	780.6	227.1	257.3	176.7	60.1	3,273.1	7,992.9	2.69
1972	1,074.0	2,270.5	782.1	243.3	267.5	208.6	59.7	3,238.3	8,139.0	·

1. Up until 1967 including cumulative turnover tax; from 1968 on without VAT and without local advertising in newspapers.
Sources: ZAW-Jahresbericht 1972, p. 87; *Media Perspektiven,* op. cit.

Section C: RADIO AND TELEVISION

TABLE 4. Revenue of radio and television corporations in 1972 (licences and advertising)

Network	DM. (millions)
State Broadcasting Services	
Revenue net from radio licences	485.2
Revenue from radio advertising agencies:	
Gross turnover	156.3
Net profit for the services	31.1
ARD	
Net revenue from television licences	654.6
Television advertising agencies	
Gross turnover	481.8
Net profit for the services	85.1
ZDF	
Net revenue from television licences	280.0
Income from television advertising	236.5

Sources: *ARD Jahrbuch, 1973*, p. 275, 311; *ZDF Jahrbuch, 1972*, p. 139.

TABLE 5. Radio and television licences: growth rate and distribution of licences per thousand inhabitants

Year	Population (000)	Radio licences			Television licences		
		Number (millions)	Growth rate over preceding year	Per 1,000 inhabitants	Number (millions)	Growth rate over preceding year	Per 1,000 inhabitants
1962	56,589	16.27	+2.4	287	5.89	+27.0	104
1963	57,247	16.70	+2.6	291	7.21	+22.5	125
1964	57,865	17.10	+2.4	295	8.54	+18.4	147
1965	58,587	17.49	+2.3	298	10.02	+17.4	171
1966	59,297	17.88	+2.2	301	11.38	+13.5	191
1967	59,793	18.23	+2.0	304	12.72	+11.8	212
1968	59,948	18.59	+1.9	310	13.81	+ 8.5	230
1969	60,463	18.99	+2.2	314	14.96	+ 8.3	247
1970	61,195	19.37	+2.0	317	15.90	+ 6.3	260
1971	61,001	19.62	+1.3	322	16.67	+ 4.9	273
1972	61,503	19.90	+1.4	324	17.43	+ 4.5	283

TABLE 6. Revenue from radio and television licences (in millions of DM.)

Year	Total receipts[1]	Of which		
		ARD	ZDF	Federal Post Office
1965	1,063.6	664.5	142.0	257.1
1966	1,152.6	707.3	157.5	287.8
1967	1,230.3	748.9	172.5	308.9
1968	1,307.3	751.3	187.1	329.6
1969	1,378.6	785.9	200.6	348.9
1970	1,726.8	1,042.8	266.5	360.1
1971	1,759.1	1,118.4	273.3	367.3
1972	1,795.2	1,139.7	280.4	375.0

1. 1968, 1969, 1970 including Value Added Tax (VAT).

TABLE 7. Radio broadcasts of the ARD Corporation 1972

ARD programmes	Broadcasting hours per year	Average broadcasting time per day
I Programme	78,602.3	214 h 46
II Programme	57,459.4	156 h 59
III Programme	39,324.5	107 h 26
Programmes for foreign workers	11,229.0	30 h 41
Advertising	14,772.5	40 h 22
TOTAL	201,387.7	550 h 14
Deutschlandfunk	11,138.7	30 h 26
Deutsche Welle	16,241.2[1]	44 h 22
GRAND TOTAL	228,767.6	625 h 03

1. To which should be added 10,309 recorded repeats.

TABLE 8. Television broadcasts of ARD and ZDF[1]

Year	ARD		ZDF	
	Broadcasting hours per year	Average broadcast time per day	Broadcasting hours per year	Average broadcast time per day
1965	2,703.3	7 h 24	2,180.4	5 h 58
1966	2,671.8	7 h 19	2,501.3	6 h 51
1967	2,675.3	7 h 20	2,594.2	7 h 06
1968	2,757.6	7 h 33	2,775.9	7 h 36
1969	2,643.5	7 h 15	2,916.0	7 h 59
1970	2,672.3	7 h 19	3,042.3	8 h 20
1971	2,677.0	7 h 20	3,134.0	8 h 35
1972	2,845.3	7 h 46	3,290.6	8 h 59

1. Not including regional programmes.

TABLE 9. Television broadcasts of the first programme of ARD, 1972

Programme content	Minutes	%	Programme content	Minutes	%
Internal productions			*National co-productions*		
Documentaries	36,619	21.5	News	16,380	9.6
Sport	2,511	1.5	Weather reports	798	0.5
Religious programmes	1,952	1.1	Weekly magazines	3,658	2.2
Television plays	18,309	10.7	Sports	5,825	3.4
Entertainment	24,204	14.2	Fiction film	14,224	8.3
Music	1,153	0.7	Entertainment film	2,195	1.3
Family programmes	19,957	11.7	Programme		
Miscellaneous	1,090	0.6	announcement	1,240	0.7
Fillers	7,992	4.7	Live sporting events	2,467	1.4
TOTAL	113,787	66.7	Olympics, Sapporo	1,687	1.0
			Olympics, Munich	6,680	3.9
			Miscellaneous	1,781	1.0
			TOTAL	56,935	33.3
			GRAND TOTAL	170,722	100.0

TABLE 10. Television broadcasts of the second programme of ZDP, 1972

Programme content	Minutes	%	Programme content	Minutes	%
Programme division			*Editing division*		
Culture	27,569	14.0	Magazines[1] and		
Television plays			special programmes	4,792	2.4
and films	41,466	21.0	Current events	28,153	14.3
Documentaries	7,516	3.8	National politics	11,246	5.7
Entertainment	17,548	8.9	Foreign politics	4,191	2.1
Theatre and music	11,645	5.9	Social policy	4,128	2.1
TOTAL	105,744	53.6	Sport	21,721	11.0
			TOTAL	74,231	37.6
Advertising	8,479	4.3			
Fillers	8,994	4.5			
TOTAL	17,473	8.8	GRAND TOTAL	197,448	100.0

1. *Bilanz, ZDF-Magazin, Kennzeichen D.*

TABLE 11. The third television programme (in minutes) of ARD[1]

Year	BR	HR	NDR/RB/ SFB	SFB[2]	WDR	SR/SDR/ SWF	Total
1964	16,590	6,936	—	—	13,442	—	36,968
1965	50,520	22,443	38,237	2,154	17,527	—	130,881
1966	53,880	35,906	42,910	2,860	76,171	—	211,727
1967	79,214	41,169	59,656	2,510	85,185	—	267,734
1968	107,123	43,631	63,140	—	86,157	—	300,051
1969	107,515	52,222	67,581	—	104,054	41,577	372,949
1970	102,198	66,992	71,416	—	130,700	69,789	441,095
1971	108,720	63,199	71,768	—	128,848	78,347	450,882
1972	116,960	74,785[3]	72,181[3]	—	138,361[3]	98,783	501,070

1. BR = Bayerische Rundfunk; HR = Hessische Rundfunk; NDR = Norddeutscher Rundfunk; RB = Radio Bremen; SFB = Sender Freies Berlin; WDR = Westdeutscher Rundfunk; SR = Saarlaendischer Rundfunk; SDR = Sueddeutscher Rundfunk; SWF = Suedwestfunk.
2. Regional broadcasts.
3. HR in addition 12,447 minutes; WDR parallel 17,883 minutes; NDR/RB/SFB in addition 22,572 minutes, all broadcast in the first TV programme.

Section D: FILM

TABLE 12. Attendance at commercial cinemas

Year	Attendance (millions)	Attendance per inhabitant	Year	Attendance (millions)	Attendance per inhabitant
1956	818	15.6	1968	179	3.0
1964	320	5.5	1969	172	2.8
1965	294	5.0	1970	160	2.6
1966	257	4.3	1971	152	2.5
1967	216	3.6	1972	150	2.4

Source: Statistical Service of SPIO.

TABLE 13. Revenue from commercial cinemas

Year	Gross revenue (DM. millions)	Entertainment tax (DM. millions)	Net revenue	Year	Gross revenue (DM. millions)	Entertainment tax (DM. millions)	Net revenue
1957	1,014	153	861	1968	523	12	511
1964	622	29	593	1969	547	12	535
1965	612	24	588	1970	543	10	533
1966	589	19	570	1971	557	7	550
1967	552	16	536	1972	576	5	571

Source: Statistical Service of SPIO.

TABLE 14. Number of commercial cinemas

Year	Cinemas	Drive-in cinemas	Year	Cinemas	Drive-in cinemas
1956	6,438	—	1968	4,060	9
1959	7,085	—	1969	3,739	17
1964	5,551	1	1970	3,446	17
1965	5,209	2	1971	3,314	19
1966	4,784	2	1972	3,171	19
1967	4,518	4			

Source: Statistical Service of SPIO.

TABLE 15. Film production (including German-foreign co-productions)

Year of production	Long films		Short films
	Feature	Documentary, social, economic	Cultural, documentary, dramatic, economic
1955	128	—	—
1958	115	22	456
1962	61	9	343
1963	66	14	252
1964	77	7	323
1965	69	7	364
1966	60	15	304
1967	96	12	315
1968	107	9	327
1969	121	17	349
1970	113	12	268
1971	93	9	201
1972	85	9	167

Source: Statistical Service of SPIO.

TABLE 16. First run films (according to country of production)

Year	Total	Federal Republic of Germany	German Democratic Republic	Austria	Switzerland	France	France/Italy	Italy	United Kingdom	United States	Japan	Others
1962	434	64	1	19	2	41	54	37	46	122	7	41
1963	409	58	—	12	4	22	58	38	49	120	6	42
1964	416	70	—	10	—	14	56	44	45	123	8	46
1965	373	56	3	6	1	19	51	38	47	111	8	33
1966	405	60	2	12	1	17	49	45	41	118	7	53
1967	432	72	2	3	—	23	41	68	56	114	11	42
1968	434	90	1	6	1	20	29	72	40	121	13	41
1969	398	114	1	1	1	19	18	51	53	99	7	34
1970	410	106	—	1	1	14	18	67	45	117	10	31
1971	385	116	—	1	4	14	26	40	23	127	8	26
1972[1]	406	119	—	2	5	21	25	52	35	102	8	37

1. Including television films.
Source: Filmstatistisches Tagebuch, SPIO, 1973.

Section E: BOOKS

TABLE 17. Book production (titles) by subject in the Federal Republic of Germany

	1961		1963		1965		1967		1969		1970	
	Titles	%	Titles	%	Titles	%	Titles	%	Titles	%	Titles	%
Universities	406	1.8	358	1.4	593	2.2	850	2.8	905	2.5	933	2.0
Religion, theology	1,481	6.4	1,747	6.8	1,661	6.1	1,489	4.9	1,930	5.4	2,831	6.0
Philosophy, phychology	495	2.1	587	2.3	692	2.3	831	2.7	862	2.4	1,024	2.2
Law, administration	1,338	5.8	1,623	6.3	1,625	6.0	1,957	6.4	2,419	6.8	2,853	6.1
Economics, social science, statistics	1,232	5.3	1,500	5.9	2,163	7.9	2,727	8.9	2,655	7.5	4,581	9.7
Politics, military affairs	263	1.1	319	1.3	471	1.7	514	1.7	884	2.5	1,056	2.2
Languages and literary studies	665	2.9	830	3.2	884	3.3	1,145	3.7	1,643	4.6	1,811	3.8
Literature	5,296	22.9	5,242	20.4	5,598	20.6	6,328	20.6	6,932	19.5	9,181	19.5
Youth books	1,109	4.8	1,355	5.3	1,285	4.7	1,327	4.3	1,141	3.2	2,330	4.9
Education, teaching	810	3.5	1,154	4.5	1,231	4.5	1,226	4.2	1,571	4.4	2,121	4.5
Youth work and school books	2,071	9.0	1,957	7.6	904	3.3	1,330	4.3	1,577	4.4	2,456	5.2
Art	688	3.0	854	3.3	1,011	3.7	933	3.0	1,259	3.5	1,549	3.3
Music, dance, theatre, Films, broadcasting	270	1.1	386	1.5	325	1.2	475	1.6	479	1.4	741	1.6
History, history of civilization, folklore	1,245	5.4	1,567	6.1	1,926	7.1	2,031	6.6	2,054	5.8	2,165	4.6
Geography, ethnology, travel	593	2.6	599	2.3	656	2.4	873	2.9	954	2.7	1,432	3.0

	No.	%	No.	%	No.	%	No.	%	No.	%	No.	%
Maps, atlases	1,097	4.7	1,225	4.3	895	3.3	903	2.9	1,303	3.7	1,306	2.8
Medicine	523	2.3	502	2.3	352	3.1	853	2.8	1,021	2.9	1,200	2.3
Natural sciences	904	3.9	1,129	4.4	1,463	5.4	1,711	5.6	2,031	5.7	2,223	4.7
Mathematics	158	0.7	176	0.7	229	0.8	287	0.9	375	1.1	355	0.3
Engineering, technology	1,090	4.7	1,112	4.3	1,411	5.2	1,380	4.5	1,826	5.1	2,309	5.1
Transportation	569	2.5	644	2.5	519	1.9	549	1.8	680	1.9	814	1.9
Agriculture and forestry, and domestic science	307	1.3	355	1.4	419	1.6	498	1.6	577	1.6	1,033	2.2
Gymnastics, sports, games	143	0.6	142	0.6	221	0.8	237	0.8	303	0.9	410	0.9
Miscellaneous	155	0.7	83	0.3	97	0.4	62	0.2	72	0.2	61	0.1
Calendars, almanacs	214	0.9	131	0.5	149	0.5	107	0.3	119	0.3	163	0.3
TOTAL	23,132	100	25,673	100	27,247	100	30,683	100	35,577	100	47,096	100

Sources: Börsenverein des Deutschen Buchhandels and calculation by the authors

Section F: USAGE OF MEDIA

TABLE 18. Coverage of television, radio and daily newspaper on
an average working day

Media usage per 100 inhabitants	Basis: total population		Basis: persons in households owning a television set	
	1964	1970	1964	1970
Television	47	72	78	82
Radio	68	67	63	68
Daily newspapers	69	70	69	72

TABLE 19. Duration of usage of media on an average working day

Time budget	Total population		Persons in households owning a television set	
	1964	1970	1964	1970
Television	1 h 10	1 h 53	1 h 58	2 h 10
Radio	1 h 29	1 h 13	1 h 11	1 h 11
Newspapers	0 h 35	0 h 35	0 h 34	0 h 35
Three media together[1]	3 h 08	3 h 34	3 h 39	3 h 50

1. If two media used at the same time only one medium is included in time budget.

TABLE 20. Percentage of population reached by media on
an average working day

Media	1964	1970
By 3 media		
Television, radio and daily newspaper	23	39
By 2 media	46	37
Of which: daily newspaper and television	(11)	(14)
daily newspaper and radio	(27)	(12)
television and radio	(8)	(11)
By one medium	24	18
Daily newspaper	(9)	(5)
Television	(5)	(8)
Radio	(10)	(5)
By none of these three media	7	5
TOTAL	100	100
Average number of media exposures	1.8	2.1